My GOD

Grant me purity of heart, so that I may honor you. With all my heart I will praise you. O Lord, my God. I will give Glory to your name forever!

Psalm 86:11-12

stephanie d. moore

Copyright © 2024 by Stephanie D. Moore

Published by
Moore Marketing and Communications, LLC

Kansas City, Missouri
StephanieDMoore.com
MooretoRead.com

In accordance with the U.S. Copyright Act of 1976, scanning, uploading, or electronic sharing of any part of this book, audio, written, or e-published is strictly prohibited and unlawful. No part of this book may be reproduced in any form by any means, including photocopying, electronic, mechanical, recording, or by any information storage and retrieval systems without permission in writing by the copyright owner.

Bulk copies or group sales of this book are available by contacting Stephanie D. Moore at moore@stephaniedmoore.com or (405) 306-9833.

Moore, Stephanie D.
My God: A 31-Day Devotional on Recognizing God's Love for Us

First Edition Printed October 2024
Printed in the USA.

Cover Design and Layout Design by
Moore Marketing and Communications, LLC.
All Rights Reserved.

> Cover Photo used in design retrieved at pexels.com, taken by gip.

ISBN: 978-1-955544-56-6

For I am the Lord your God, who stirs up the sea
so that its waves roar—the Lord Almighty is his name.
I have put my words in your mouth and covered you with the
shadow of my hand—I who set the heavens in place,

my GOD

Introduction		9
Day 1	Be Holy As I am Holy	15
Day 2	To Please God	21
Day 3	Wisdom and Discernment from God	25
Day 4	God Reveals Wisdom	29
Day 5	At God's Command	33
Day 6	An Aroma Pleasing Unto the Lord	37
Day 7	Blessing and Vindication	43
Day 8	Living Water	47
Day 9	Take Heed, Fear Not, and Be Quiet	51
Day 10	Sing to the Lord	55
Day 11	Consider What He Said	59
Day 12	Daybreak	63
Day 13	See and Say	67
Day 14	Perseverance is Victory	71
Day 15	His Glory Shall Be Seen Upon Thee	75
Day 16	Wherever I Go	81
Day 17	Under His Wings	87
Day 18	In His Hands	91
Day 19	Identity Crisis	95
Day 20	For Those We Serve	101
Day 21	The Good Shepherd	105
Day 22	The Lord Will Answer	113
Day 23	Separate & Protected	117
Day 24	Run	123
Day 25	Consider, ASK, and Be Wise	127
Day 26	As God Commands	133
Day 27	The Cause was of God	137
Day 28	Day and Night	141
Day 29	Where is Your God?	145
Day 30	It's Easier to Start a War than End One	149
Day 31	Make His Praise Glorious!	155

stephanie d. moore

In Loving Memory

Allan "Grip" Smith

*We always triumph through Christ
when people witness the effect
of the knowledge of Christ in our lives
everywhere we go.*

2 Corinthians 2:14

Introduction

*The grass withers and the flowers fall, but the
word of our God endures forever.*
Isaiah 40:8

God isn't going to change, neither is he going anywhere. As the various cultures of the world attempt to claim there is no God or to redefine Him, I realize every day, just how wrong they are in doing so.

We are blessed to have an environment with blue skies, green trees, the earth beneath our feet, and air we can breathe. We live in an environment that was created to sustain life and we

My GOD

must acknowledge none of us were born with the knowledge to create the world we live in. God, the creator of heaven and earth, loves us immensely and stands afar to see if anyone will seek him, acknowledge him, or even try to understand who he truly is. He sent his son, Jesus Christ, to be God with us, and has left his Holy Spirit to be God within us.

When I realized that we serve a living God, who hears us, listens, and loves each of us - uniquely and individually, it changed my life. God is knocking at the door of our hearts to see if we will let him in. He desires to be Your God, just as he is My God.

I want to pray more, and with clear direction. I want to sacrifice my will for his will. I want to be more intentional in my generosity. I want the work that I do with my hands to align with his purpose for my life.

Most importantly, I want to be closer to God than I have ever desired to be. I love the Lord, and I know without a doubt, that he loves me. I know that he only desires the best for my life.

I NEED A SPIRITUAL CLEANSING, A NEW OUTLOOK, A NEW WINE SKIN, A NEW HEART, A NEW ATTITUDE, AND A NEW ADDRESS. I WANT TO FIND MYSELF CONNECTED TO GOD IN A WAY I HAVE NEVER BEEN BEFORE. MY HOPE IS THAT BY READING THIS BOOK, YOU TOO WILL DEVELOP THIS THIRST OR HUNGER TO KNOW GOD IN A GREATER WAY.

I realized a long time ago, that God is the key, the answer, the King of Kings, the Lord of Lords. I am grateful for the sacrifice of Jesus Christ, who is my Savior, the one and true living God. I am praying to be endowed by the Holy Spirit, that I may represent God in the spaces I am in. I am praying that I decrease as he increases.

I thank God for his love, his mercy, and his grace.

For I am the Lord your God, who stirs up the sea so that its waves roar—the Lord Almighty is his name. I have put my words in your mouth and covered you with the shadow of my hand— I who set the heavens in place, who laid the foundations of the earth, and who say to Zion, 'You are my people.'

Isaiah 51:15-16

Daily Prayer

Most Gracious and Heavenly Father,

I love the Lord, my God, with all my heart and with all my soul and with all my strength and with all my mind, and I love my neighbor as myself. Luke 10:27
On the glorious splendor of your majesty and on your wonderful works, I meditate. Psalm 145:5

As the deer pants for water, so I long for you, O God. I thirst for God, the living God. Where can I find him to come and stand before him? Psalm 42:1-2

But you, Lord, are a shield around me; you are my glory, the one who holds my head high. Psalm 3:3 *You perform great and wonderful deeds, for you alone are God. Teach me your ways, O Lord, that I may live according to your truth! Grant me purity of heart, so that I may honor you. With all my heart I will praise you. O Lord, my God. I will give Glory to your name forever!*
Psalm 86:10-12

I know just what to do for God has made me see and understand. Isaiah 28:26

O give thanks to the Lord, for he is good; for his mercy endures forever. Let the redeemed of the Lord say so, whom he has redeemed from the hand of the enemy and gathered out of the lands, from the east and from the west, from the north and from the south. They wandered in the wilderness in a solitary way, they found no city to dwell in. Hungry and thirsty, their soul fainted in them. Then they cried unto the Lord in their trouble and he delivered them out of their distresses. And he led them forth by the right way, that they might go to a city of habitation. Oh that men would praise the Lord for his goodness, and his wonderful works to the children of men.
Psalm 107:1-8

For yours, O Lord, is the greatness and the power and the glory and the victory and the majesty, for all that is in the heavens and in the earth is yours. Yours is the kingdom, O Lord, you are exalted as head above all.
1 Chronicles 29:11

In Jesus' Name, Amen

Be Holy as I am Holy

And thou shalt make holy garments for Aaron thy brother for glory and for beauty.

And thou shalt speak unto all that are wise hearted, whom I have filled with the spirit of wisdom, that they may make Aaron's garments to consecrate him, that he may minister unto me in the priest's office.

Exodus 28:2-3

There is a unique responsibility on those who have been elected to share the good news of Jesus Christ with others. The importance of such work is amplified in the Old Testament, Exodus 28.

THE DETAILS MATTER. GOD IS LOOKING FOR A MINISTER THAT WILL BE HOLY AS HE IS HOLY, BECAUSE ONLY THEN

GOD

ARE YOU PREPARED TO RECEIVE AND SHARE WHAT GOD PLACES ON YOUR HEART. THE GARMENTS THAT ARE PREPARED FOR THE PRIEST, AARON AND HIS SONS, THE LEVITES WERE CREATED TO BRING GOD GLORY AND TO REFLECT THE BEAUTY OF WHAT THEY WERE TO BECOME, VESSELS FOR GOD.

And before they were released to minister to others, their first responsibility was to minister to God. God had specific items of clothing, and specific requirements for them prior to entering his presence. Secondly, these items were to only be created by those who had the Spirit of Wisdom.

> And these are the garments which they shall make; a breastplate, and an ephod, and a robe, and a broidered coat, a mitre, and a girdle: and they shall make holy garments for Aaron thy brother, and his sons, that he may minister unto me in the priest's office.
>
> Exodus 28:4

There is a reason God expects us to consecrate ourselves for his use. Yesterday, I started a fast that literally ended with a promise that I made to my friend to go to Bingo with her at the local VFW, a Monday activity we often partake in a couple of weeks each month. We will get our favorite snacks and a hot meal and settle in for an evening of cheap thrills with good friends (regulars at the hall and the workers who volunteer their time). It is always fun, but it was not where I was supposed to be nor what I was supposed to be doing. In my head and heart, I knew I was on the wrong path but it was difficult to tell my desires no. Of course, we didn't win and when I got home, I read Exodus 28.

This is where God led me. God knows I want to be close to him for this book, especially, as it relates to him being "My God" and your God. There is a level of intimacy I would like to share with God to assist me in delivering the message that he desires.

So, yesterday, after the thrills had been had, God placed me squarely back into reality. Though the blood of Christ has ripped the vail between God and I, there is still a cost and consecration required to enter into the Holy of Holies. It does not mean that God will not hear my prayers, of God forbid should something

bad happen today that I would not go to heaven, but it does mean that the revelation that God gives to his priests is revealed when our hearts and minds are focused solely on him and his will. Only then can we reflect the glory and the beauty of God as a vessel of his messages and acts.

MY GOD REQUIRES THAT I AM HOLY AS HE IS HOLY TO RECEIVE A REVELATION THAT WILL BE BRING GLORY AND BEAUTY AND ALLOW ME TO MINISTER IN HIS PRESENCE. THIS REQUIRES A SPIRIT OF WISDOM AND A WISE HEART THAT GOD GIVES TO THOSE WHO WILL PAY ATTENTION TO DETAIL AND TAKE RESPONSIBILITY.

Daily Prayer

Most Gracious and Heavenly Father,

I love the Lord, my God, with all my heart and with all my soul and with all my strength and with all my mind, and I love my neighbor as myself. Luke 10:27 *On the glorious splendor of your majesty and on your wonderful works, I meditate.* Psalm 145:5

As the deer pants for water, so I long for you, O God. I thirst for God, the living God. Where can I find him to come and stand before him? Psalm 42: 1-2

But you, Lord, are a shield around me; you are my glory, the one who holds my head high. Psalm 3:3 *You perform great and wonderful deeds, for you alone are God. Teach me your ways, O Lord, that I may live according to your truth! Grant me purity of heart, so that I may honor you. With all my heart I will praise you. O Lord, my God. I will give Glory to your name forever!*
Psalm 86:10-12

I know just what to do for God has made me see and understand. Isaiah 28:26

O give thanks to the Lord, for he is good; for his mercy endures forever. Let the redeemed of the Lord say so, whom he has redeemed from the hand of the enemy and gathered out of the lands, from the east and from the west, from the north and from the south. They wandered in the wilderness in a solitary way, they found no city to dwell in. Hungry and thirsty, their soul fainted in them. Then they cried unto the Lord in their trouble and he delivered them out of their distresses. And he led them forth by the right way, that they might go to a city of habitation. Oh that men would praise the Lord for his goodness, and his wonderful works to the children of men.
Psalm 107:1-8

For yours, O Lord, is the greatness and the power and the glory and the victory and the majesty, for all that is in the heavens and in the earth is yours. Yours is the kingdom, O Lord, you are exalted as head above all.
I Chronicles 29:11

In Jesus' Name, Amen

To Please God

Joash tried hard to please the Lord all during the lifetime of Jehoiada the priest.

But after his death, the leaders of Judah came to King Joash and induced him to abandon the Temple of the God of their ancestors and to worship shameful idols instead! So the wrath of God came down upon Judah and Jerusalem again. God sent prophets to bring them back to the Lord, but the people wouldn't listen.

Then the Spirit of God came upon Zechariah, Jehoiada's son. He called a meeting of all the people. Standing before them upon a platform, he said to them, "God wants to know why you are disobeying his commandments. For when you do, everything you try fails. You have forsaken the Lord, and now he has forsaken you." Then the leaders plotted to kill Zechariah, and finally King Joash himself ordered him executed in the court of the Temple. That was how King Joash repaid Jehoiada for his love and loyalty—by killing his son. Zechariah's last words as he died were, "Lord, see what they are doing and pay them back."

2 Chronicles 24:2, 18-22

God

It is very important that our worship of God is to pursue an authentic and genuine relationship with the Lord. Early in his career, it appears as though a young Joash realized this. It is evidenced by his personal actions when the high priest did not render the results he desired in directing the Levites to pursue the temple tax to rebuild the house of God. Instead, Joash took matters into his own hands and sent a proclamation under his kingship to all of the counties which generated great results.

Yet, after many years of peace and worship in his land, when the high priest Jehoida passed away, Joash was easily led astray. There could be many reasons for this, as a disruption in activity can sometimes be a welcome change, but we must be careful what we allow to entertain us in the absence of creativity and ingenuity. King Joash's choices would lead to his downfall.

Not only did he ignore the warnings of God as provided by his prophets, but he also ordered the death of Jehoida's son (because the message he brought was not good news but the voice of conviction). Rather than accept his error and turn about, King Joash doubled down converting his conviction to condemnation and cursed not only his own life but also the lives of those who served him faithfully.

His kingdom was destroyed by a small Syrian army empowered by God. Later, Joash was killed in his bed by those who loved Jehoida the priest, and carried out the vengeance of his son. Joash was not buried among the honorable kings, simply in the city of David.

MY GOD REQUIRES THAT WE AUTHENTICALLY DESIRE TO PLEASE HIM AND HIM ALONE, ONLY THEN CAN WE SEE, AND MAINTAIN GREAT SUCCESS, AND HONOR BEFORE HIM.

Daily Prayer

Most Gracious and Heavenly Father,

I love the Lord, my God, with all my heart and with all my soul and with all my strength and with all my mind, and I love my neighbor as myself. Luke 10:27 On the glorious splendor of your majesty and on your wonderful works, I meditate. Psalm 145:5

As the deer pants for water, so I long for you, O God. I thirst for God, the living God. Where can I find him to come and stand before him? Psalm 42: 1-2

But you, Lord, are a shield around me; you are my glory, the one who holds my head high. Psalm 3:3 You perform great and wonderful deeds, for you alone are God. Teach me your ways, O Lord, that I may live according to your truth! Grant me purity of heart, so that I may honor you. With all my heart I will praise you. O Lord, my God. I will give Glory to your name forever! Psalm 86:10-12

I know just what to do for God has made me see and understand. Isaiah 28:26

O give thanks to the Lord, for he is good; for his mercy endures forever. Let the redeemed of the Lord say so, whom he has redeemed from the hand of the enemy and gathered out of the lands, from the east and from the west, from the north and from the south. They wandered in the wilderness in a solitary way, they found no city to dwell in. Hungry and thirsty, their soul fainted in them. Then they cried unto the Lord in their trouble and he delivered them out of their distresses. And he led them forth by the right way, that they might go to a city of habitation. Oh that men would praise the Lord for his goodness, and his wonderful works to the children of men. Psalm 107:1-8

For yours, O Lord, is the greatness and the power and the glory and the victory and the majesty, for all that is in the heavens and in the earth is yours. Yours is the kingdom, O Lord, you are exalted as head above all. I Chronicles 29:11

In Jesus' Name, Amen

mooretoread.com

Day 3

Wisdom and Discernment from God

And Solomon loved the Lord, walking in the statutes of David his father: only he sacrificed and burnt incense in high places.

And now, O Lord my God, thou hast made thy servant king instead of David my father: and I am but a little child: I know not how to go out or come in.

And thy servant is in the midst of thy people which thou hast chosen, a great people, that cannot be numbered nor counted for multitude.

Give therefore thy servant an understanding heart to judge thy people, that I may discern between good and bad: for who is able to judge this thy so great a people?

And the speech pleased the Lord, that Solomon had asked this thing.

I Kings 3:3, 7-10

My GOD

Knowledge obtained through education, skill sets, or mentorship often prove to be invaluable, but there is knowledge we can only receive from God. The personal knowledge we receive from Our Father in Heaven, is Rhema knowledge - wisdom and discernment. It is personal, it meets us where we are and provides for us a unique advantage.

King Solomon was crowned king at a very young age, and he realized the great weight that was placed upon him. He loved the Lord with all of his heart, his mind, and his being. He also wanted to walk well in the footsteps of his father David.

King Solomon's heart was in the right place. He greatly desired to honor God, the position he was placed in, and to serve well. Because his heart was right, God elevated him with wisdom, discernment, honor, and wealth.

Before King Solomon requested knowledge, he worshipped

God. He also admitted that he didn't know everything. He didn't have all of the answers. He needed God's help!

Humility is a strength. Honor comes from God. When we seek God with all of our hearts and let him know that He is our priority, and that His will and His way is our desire - God answers our prayer.

MY GOD WILL SUPPLY AN ABUNDANCE OF WISDOM, DISCERNMENT, HONOR, AND WEALTH TO THOSE WHO SEEK HIS FACE AND NOT HIS HAND.

WHEN WE COME TO GOD IN HUMILITY, SINCERITY, AND A PURE HEART HE ENDOWS US WITH A RHEMA WISDOM THAT ONLY GOD CAN PROVIDE.

Daily Prayer

Most Gracious and Heavenly Father,

I love the Lord, my God, with all my heart and with all my soul and with all my strength and with all my mind, and I love my neighbor as myself. Luke 10:27 *On the glorious splendor of your majesty and on your wonderful works, I meditate.* Psalm 145:5

As the deer pants for water, so I long for you, O God. I thirst for God, the living God. Where can I find him to come and stand before him? Psalm 42:1-2

But you, Lord, are a shield around me; you are my glory, the one who holds my head high. Psalm 3:3 *You perform great and wonderful deeds, for you alone are God. Teach me your ways, O Lord, that I may live according to your truth! Grant me purity of heart, so that I may honor you. With all my heart I will praise you. O Lord, my God. I will give Glory to your name forever!* Psalm 86:10-12

I know just what to do for God has made me see and understand. Isaiah 28:26

O give thanks to the Lord, for he is good; for his mercy endures forever. Let the redeemed of the Lord say so, whom he has redeemed from the hand of the enemy and gathered out of the lands, from the east and from the west, from the north and from the south. They wandered in the wilderness in a solitary way, they found no city to dwell in. Hungry and thirsty, their soul fainted in them. Then they cried unto the Lord in their trouble and he delivered them out of their distresses. And he led them forth by the right way, that they might go to a city of habitation. Oh that men would praise the Lord for his goodness, and his wonderful works to the children of men. Psalm 107:1-8

For yours, O Lord, is the greatness and the power and the glory and the victory and the majesty, for all that is in the heavens and in the earth is yours. Yours is the kingdom, O Lord, you are exalted as head above all. I Chronicles 29:11

In Jesus' Name, Amen

God Reveals Wisdom

So these three men stopped answering Job, because he was righteous in his own eyes. But Elihu son of Barakel the Buzite, of the family of Ram, became very angry with Job for justifying himself rather than God.

Job 32: 1-2

Even with the best intentions to live a life worthy of God's calling, we fail - miserably. Job, who lived an honorable life before God and lost all he valued in a matter of days was left with this stark realization to ponder upon.

When Job lost it all, his friends assumed it was his fault. They assumed that Job was at the center of his loss, the cause of

his loss, and that he was living in secret sin. But in reality, God chose Job to experience hardship because no matter his plight, Job would always honor and put God first.

But in his own error, Job did not realize complaining about his situation was also a sin, even if it were no fault of his own. Why? God, the creator of all things, is in control. In God's eyes, we may experience unfair situations but God is in control of all and he only chooses what is best for us.

When times get rocky, and seem to make little sense, we must lean on the knowledge that God is in control and that this too shall pass. It seems harder to do than it is to say, but God promises that if we keep our mind stayed on him, he will keep us in perfect peace.

This is what God desired of Job. God wanted Job to reflect the goodness of the Lord in spite of his situation. For in this perspective lies the cornerstone of wisdom, to recognize who God is regardless of what we experience. We are to trust God when we cannot trace him and to know, he is aware, available, and willing to help us in our time of need.

MY GOD KNOWS ALL THAT CONCERNS ME, ALL THAT I CARRY. REGARDLESS OF MY CIRCUMSTANCE, I KNOW THAT MY GOD IS GOOD AND HE LOVES ME WITHOUT BOUNDARY.

Daily Prayer

Most Gracious and Heavenly Father,

I love the Lord, my God, with all my heart and with all my soul and with all my strength and with all my mind, and I love my neighbor as myself. Luke 10:27
On the glorious splendor of your majesty and on your wonderful works, I meditate. Psalm 145:5

As the deer pants for water, so I long for you, O God. I thirst for God, the living God. Where can I find him to come and stand before him? Psalm 42:1-2

But you, Lord, are a shield around me; you are my glory, the one who holds my head high. Psalm 3:3 *You perform great and wonderful deeds, for you alone are God. Teach me your ways, O Lord, that I may live according to your truth! Grant me purity of heart, so that I may honor you. With all my heart I will praise you. O Lord, my God. I will give Glory to your name forever!*
Psalm 86:10-12

I know just what to do for God has made me see and understand. Isaiah 28:26

O give thanks to the Lord, for he is good; for his mercy endures forever. Let the redeemed of the Lord say so, whom he has redeemed from the hand of the enemy and gathered out of the lands, from the east and from the west, from the north and from the south. They wandered in the wilderness in a solitary way, they found no city to dwell in. Hungry and thirsty, their soul fainted in them. Then they cried unto the Lord in their trouble and he delivered them out of their distresses. And he led them forth by the right way, that they might go to a city of habitation. Oh that men would praise the Lord for his goodness, and his wonderful works to the children of men.
Psalm 107:1-8

For yours, O Lord, is the greatness and the power and the glory and the victory and the majesty, for all that is in the heavens and in the earth is yours. Yours is the kingdom, O Lord, you are exalted as head above all.
I Chronicles 29:11

In Jesus' Name, Amen

Day 5

At God's Command

By faith we understand that the universe was formed at God's command, so that what is seen was not made out of what was visible.

Hebrews 11:2

When God created the world we know, he did so by faith and his command. In the same way, we are to believe, confess, act, and expect. But there is a unique message (beyond our traditional faith message) shared in Hebrews 11.

1. Faith does not mean we will personally see our hopes come to pass, it may be for those that come after us.
2. This does not mean that we should not believe, confess, act, and expect it to come to pass while we are living.

3. Even though we may be gone, our actions and confessions of faith will allow us to live on.

> Therefore, brothers and sisters, since we have confidence to enter the Most Holy Place by the blood of Jesus, by a new and living way opened for us through the curtain, that is, his body, and since we have a great priest over the house of God, let us draw near to God with a sincere heart and with the full assurance that faith brings, having our hearts sprinkled to cleanse us from a guilty conscience and having our bodies washed with pure water. Let us hold unswervingly to the hope we profess, for he who promised is faithful.
>
> Hebrews 10:19-23

JESUS CHRIST IS THE AUTHOR AND FINISHER OF OUR FAITH. HE BELIEVED IN FAITH TO THE COMMAND OF GOD, AND DID AS GOD INSTRUCTED. HE DID NOT SEE THE PROMISE FULFILLED BEFORE HE SACRIFICED HIS LIFE FOR US, BUT HE BELIEVED AND THEREFORE WE ARE BENEFICIARIES OF HIS FAITH.

In the same way, Abel still speaks [Hebrews 11:4], Noah saved humanity [Hebrews 11:7], Moses sacrificed his royal stature [Hebrews 11:26], and Rahab was in the bloodline of Jesus Christ because she had faith in God and obeyed the command [Hebrews 11:31].

These were all commended for their faith, yet none of them received what had been promised, since God had planned something better for us so that only together with us would they be made perfect.

Hebrews 11:39

MY GOD HAS DESIGNED THE BEGINNING FROM THE END AND KNOWS THE PATH WE SHOULD ALL TAKE. ALL WE MUST DO IS BELIEVE, CONFESS, ACT, AND EXPECT IT TO COME TO PASS.

Daily Prayer

Most Gracious and Heavenly Father,

I love the Lord, my God, with all my heart and with all my soul and with all my strength and with all my mind, and I love my neighbor as myself. *Luke 10:27* On the glorious splendor of your majesty and on your wonderful works, I meditate. *Psalm 145:5*

As the deer pants for water, so I long for you, O God. I thirst for God, the living God. Where can I find him to come and stand before him? *Psalm 42: 1-2*

But you, Lord, are a shield around me; you are my glory, the one who holds my head high. *Psalm 3:3* You perform great and wonderful deeds, for you alone are God. Teach me your ways, O Lord, that I may live according to your truth! Grant me purity of heart, so that I may honor you. With all my heart I will praise you. O Lord, my God. I will give Glory to your name forever!
Psalm 86:10-12

I know just what to do for God has made me see and understand. *Isaiah 28:26*

O give thanks to the Lord, for he is good; for his mercy endures forever. Let the redeemed of the Lord say so, whom he has redeemed from the hand of the enemy and gathered out of the lands, from the east and from the west, from the north and from the south. They wandered in the wilderness in a solitary way, they found no city to dwell in. Hungry and thirsty, their soul fainted in them. Then they cried unto the Lord in their trouble and he delivered them out of their distresses. And he led them forth by the right way, that they might go to a city of habitation. Oh that men would praise the Lord for his goodness, and his wonderful works to the children of men.
Psalm 107:1-8

For yours, O Lord, is the greatness and the power and the glory and the victory and the majesty, for all that is in the heavens and in the earth is yours. Yours is the kingdom, O Lord, you are exalted as head above all.
I Chronicles 29:11

In Jesus' Name, Amen

mooretoread.com

An Aroma Pleasing Unto the Lord

It is a burnt offering, a food offering, an aroma pleasing to the Lord.

Leviticus 1:9b

When God asks us to do something, he has a good reason for doing so. His ways are not our ways. But following (his directions) is an aroma that is pleasing to the Lord.

An offering was given to atone for sin, and the specification of steps to render the offering mattered as much as the offering itself.

 **GOD**

> In fact, obedience is described as an aroma pleasing to the Lord.

Sins are the result of paths we have taken because we don't trust the guidance of God - to do it his way. The atonement process indicates through our actions that we are returning to God, to do his will, in his specified way. The atonement is not desired by God because he needs us to operate like robots that simply do his bidding, it is an illustration of trust.

> When we are betrayed by those we love, it hurts us deeply and our trust erodes. Our desire to be in their presence lessens and we pull away. This is God's reaction to us when we pull away as well.

Give glory to the Lord your God before he brings the darkness, before your feet stumble on the darkening hills. You hope for light, but he will turn it to utter darkness and change it to deep gloom. If you do not listen, I will weep in secret because of your pride; my eyes will weep bitterly, overflowing with tears, because the Lord's flock will be taken captive. Say to the king and to the queen mother, "Come down from your thrones, for your glorious crowns will fall from your heads."

Jeremiah 13:16-18

God gave Moses the instructions for the people who wished to atone for their sins. He provided a way to return and restore a relationship with him. As we walk down our paths of life, God also illustrates this to us in demonstrative ways. As our personal relationships sour or take a turn for the worst, it shines a light on our relationship with God. How are we responding to his desire? His will?

When a man's ways please the Lord, he maketh even his enemies to be at peace with him.

Proverbs 16:7

Obedience brings trust, trust brings friendship. God is our friend, the best friend we can and will ever have. He loves us immensely and desires to bless us. Our obedience to God and our prioritization of his will brings with it peace, confidence, and love.

Jesus gave his life that we may have restoration with God without our performance of the detailed atonement process described in Leviticus 1. Instead, Jesus was the unblemished lamb of God, sacrificed that we may have life and have it more abundantly.

MY GOD IS MY FRIEND, MY ROCK, MY SHIELD, AND MY EXCEEDING GREAT REWARD. HE DESIRES TO BE IN A HEALTHY RELATIONSHIP WITH ME AND ALLOWS FOR A MERCIFUL PATH TO RESTORATION EACH MORNING.

Daily Prayer

Most Gracious and Heavenly Father,

I love the Lord, my God, with all my heart and with all my soul and with all my strength and with all my mind, and I love my neighbor as myself. Luke 10:27
On the glorious splendor of your majesty and on your wonderful works, I meditate. Psalm 145:5

As the deer pants for water, so I long for you, O God. I thirst for God, the living God. Where can I find him to come and stand before him? Psalm 42:1-2

But you, Lord, are a shield around me; you are my glory, the one who holds my head high. Psalm 3:3 *You perform great and wonderful deeds, for you alone are God. Teach me your ways, O Lord, that I may live according to your truth! Grant me purity of heart, so that I may honor you. With all my heart I will praise you. O Lord, my God. I will give Glory to your name forever!*
Psalm 86:10-12

I know just what to do for God has made me see and understand. Isaiah 28:26

O give thanks to the Lord, for he is good; for his mercy endures forever. Let the redeemed of the Lord say so, whom he has redeemed from the hand of the enemy and gathered out of the lands, from the east and from the west, from the north and from the south. They wandered in the wilderness in a solitary way, they found no city to dwell in. Hungry and thirsty, their soul fainted in them. Then they cried unto the Lord in their trouble and he delivered them out of their distresses. And he led them forth by the right way, that they might go to a city of habitation. Oh that men would praise the Lord for his goodness, and his wonderful works to the children of men.
Psalm 107:1-8

For yours, O Lord, is the greatness and the power and the glory and the victory and the majesty, for all that is in the heavens and in the earth is yours. Yours is the kingdom, O Lord, you are exalted as head above all.
I Chronicles 29:11

In Jesus' Name, Amen

Day 7

Blessing and Vindication

They will receive blessing from the Lord and vindication from God their Savior. Such is the generation of those who seek him, who seek your face, God of Jacob.

Psalm 24:5-6

Judgment is reserved for God alone. The Lord created all things, there is nothing that was created that was not created by him. Therefore, when we worship false idols, like material objects, power, wealth, or position, we are manuevering to obtain a facet of God's infinite wisdom without acknowledging the creator himself.

MY GOD

But when we seek God and place him first, we are endowed with innumerable non-negotiable blessings and are led into an abundant life we did not seek or even know to ask for. Moreover, we are blessed with the presence of God.

GOD IS FAR GREATER THAN ANY PERSON WE MAY KNOW. WHEN WE ARE EXPECTING COMPANY, WE CLEAN, PREPARE, AND DESIRE TO ENSURE OUR GUEST HAS A GOOD TIME IN OUR PRESENCE. AS A SOCIETY, WE ARE ESPECIALLY INGRATIATING TO DIGNITARIES THAT MAY ENTER OUR HOME.

"Here I am! I stand at the door and knock. If anyone hears my voice and opens the door, I will come in and eat with that person, and they with me. To the one who is victorious, I will give the right to sit with me on my throne, just as I was victorious and sat down with my Father on his throne. Whoever has ears, let them hear what the Spirit says to the churches."

Revelation 3:20-22

When we walk with intentionality, purpose, and a relentless nature to honor every moment we may spend in the presence of God, we receive blessings and vindication. Our vindication is the evidence of God on our lives. When others begin to question our loyalty to God or why we worship the way we do, God is faithful. Not only will he prepare a table for us in the presence of our enemies, he will rescue us from the enemies snare and enact vengeance on our behalf.

Lift up your heads, you gates; be lifted up, you ancient doors, that the King of glory may come in. Who is this King of glory? The Lord strong and mighty, the Lord mighty in battle. Lift up your heads, you gates; lift them up, you ancient doors, that the King of glory may come in.

Psalm 24: 7-9

MY GOD IS WITH ME EVERY MOMENT AND I BASK IN HIS PRESENCE. RATHER THAN SEEK THE DESIRES OF THIS WORLD, MY JOY IS IN HIS PRESENCE, MY AWARD IS HIS FAITHFULNESS, HE IS MY BLESSING AND MY VINDICATION FOR MY LIVING IS NOT IN VAIN.

Daily Prayer

Most Gracious and Heavenly Father,

I love the Lord, my God, with all my heart and with all my soul and with all my strength and with all my mind, and I love my neighbor as myself. Luke 10:27
On the glorious splendor of your majesty and on your wonderful works, I meditate. Psalm 145:5

As the deer pants for water, so I long for you, O God. I thirst for God, the living God. Where can I find him to come and stand before him? Psalm 42:1-2

But you, Lord, are a shield around me; you are my glory, the one who holds my head high. Psalm 3:3 *You perform great and wonderful deeds, for you alone are God. Teach me your ways, O Lord, that I may live according to your truth! Grant me purity of heart, so that I may honor you. With all my heart I will praise you. O Lord, my God. I will give Glory to your name forever!*
Psalm 86:10-12

I know just what to do for God has made me see and understand. Isaiah 28:26

O give thanks to the Lord, for he is good; for his mercy endures forever. Let the redeemed of the Lord say so, whom he has redeemed from the hand of the enemy and gathered out of the lands, from the east and from the west, from the north and from the south. They wandered in the wilderness in a solitary way, they found no city to dwell in. Hungry and thirsty, their soul fainted in them. Then they cried unto the Lord in their trouble and he delivered them out of their distresses. And he led them forth by the right way, that they might go to a city of habitation. Oh that men would praise the Lord for his goodness, and his wonderful works to the children of men.
Psalm 107:1-8

For yours, O Lord, is the greatness and the power and the glory and the victory and the majesty, for all that is in the heavens and in the earth is yours. Yours is the kingdom, O Lord, you are exalted as head above all.
I Chronicles 29:11

In Jesus' Name, Amen

Day 8

Living Water

"Whoever believes in me, as Scripture has said, rivers of living water will flow from within them."

John 7:38

The Word of God is effective and relevant, useful for teaching today. But the Holy Spirit which is from God cannot readily be interpreted, geographically identified, or regulated within the confinement of opinions or facts. When Jesus tells the crowd that anyone who comes to him, and believes in him will receive living water, he is referencing the Holy Spirit.

Jesus is and was before anything that was created came to be. He is the Living Word, Emmanuel, God with us, the King of

# MY GOD

Kings and the Lord of Lords. But Jesus has also given a special gift to each of us who choose to accept him as our Lord and Savior, and that gift is the Holy Spirit.

> THE HOLY SPIRIT NOT ONLY ALLOWS US TO HEAR WITH CLARITY GOD'S VOICE IN EVERY DAY MOMENTS, BUT HE ALSO REVEALS TO US THOSE THINGS WHICH CAN BE AND ARE DANGEROUS TO US. THE HOLY SPIRIT GIVES US REVELATION, AND THE POWER TO HARVEST FRUIT THAT SHALL REMAIN. WE ARE EMPOWERED TO PLANT SEEDS OF CURIOSITY AS IT RELATES TO HOLINESS AND RIGHTEOUSNESS IN THOSE AROUND US AND WE CAN SHARE IN UNIQUE WAYS THE MANIFESTATION OF JESUS CHRIST IN REAL TIME. WE ARE THE HANDS AND FEET OF CHRIST.

Therefore, it is important that we realize that rivers of living water will flow from within us. For each of us, it flows differently. For some the Holy Spirit will speak in songs or hymnals, others through storytelling or demonstration, for yet others through preaching and teaching, and still others through acts of kindness and love. No matter how the Holy Spirit chooses to manifest the love of God through us, he will do so abundantly. There will not be a little bit of it, but an abundance of wisdom, grace, mercy, love, patience, resilience and righteousness.

MY GOD WILL FLOW FROM WITHIN ME BY THE POWER OF THE HOLY SPIRIT AND HIS VOICE WILL BE AMPLIFIED AND MAGNIFIED AMONG THOSE WHO ARE IN ITS PRESENCE.

Daily Prayer

Most Gracious and Heavenly Father,

I love the Lord, my God, with all my heart and with all my soul and with all my strength and with all my mind, and I love my neighbor as myself. *Luke 10:27* On the glorious splendor of your majesty and on your wonderful works, I meditate. *Psalm 145:5*

As the deer pants for water, so I long for you, O God. I thirst for God, the living God. Where can I find him to come and stand before him? *Psalm 42: 1-2*

But you, Lord, are a shield around me; you are my glory, the one who holds my head high. *Psalm 3:3* You perform great and wonderful deeds, for you alone are God. Teach me your ways, O Lord, that I may live according to your truth! Grant me purity of heart, so that I may honor you. With all my heart I will praise you. O Lord, my God. I will give Glory to your name forever!
Psalm 86:10-12

I know just what to do for God has made me see and understand. *Isaiah 28:26*

O give thanks to the Lord, for he is good; for his mercy endures forever. Let the redeemed of the Lord say so, whom he has redeemed from the hand of the enemy and gathered out of the lands, from the east and from the west, from the north and from the south. They wandered in the wilderness in a solitary way, they found no city to dwell in. Hungry and thirsty, their soul fainted in them. Then they cried unto the Lord in their trouble and he delivered them out of their distresses. And he led them forth by the right way, that they might go to a city of habitation. Oh that men would praise the Lord for his goodness, and his wonderful works to the children of men.
Psalm 107:1-8

For yours, O Lord, is the greatness and the power and the glory and the victory and the majesty, for all that is in the heavens and in the earth is yours. Yours is the kingdom, O Lord, you are exalted as head above all.
1 Chronicles 29:11

In Jesus' Name, Amen

mooretoread.com

Day 9

Take Heed and Be Quiet, Fear Not

"Say to him, 'Be careful, keep calm and don't be afraid. Do not lose heart...'"

Isaiah 7:4a

King Ahaz was under attack. Two powerful kings had joined forces and plotted to destroy the kingdom of Judah. But God told him that the plot of his enemy would not succeed.

This specific scripture is written various ways in different versions of the Bible, but I truly appreciate them all and think hearing each helps to paint a clear picture of what God was telling King Ahaz.

MY GOD

> "And say unto him, 'Take heed, and be quiet; fear not, neither be fainthearted...'" (KJV)

> "Tell Ahaz to stop worrying. There's no need for him to be afraid..." (CEV)

> "Tell him, Listen, calm down. Don't be afraid. And don't panic..." (MSG)

> "Tell him to stop worrying. Tell him he doesn't need to fear..." (NLT)

Even when another nation (Ephraim) joined forces with the two kings who vowed to destroy Judah, God told King Ahaz that all would be well. But he also told him something very important, that if he did not believe, his kingdom would not be established. This statement is also worth exploring in the various versions of the Bible.

> "Unless your faith is firm, I cannot make you stand firm." (NLT)

> "If you don't take your stand in faith, you won't have a leg to stand on." (MSG)

> "And if Ahaz and his officials don't trust me, they will be defeated." (CEV)

> "If ye will not believe, surely ye shall not be established." (KJV)

> "If you do not stand firm in your faith, you will not stand at all.'" (NIV)

But God also, gave us an unwavering sign, that the battle is not ours, it belongs to God. He sent us Jesus Christ - Immanuel, God with us. You see, we have a God that never sleeps nor slumbers. He sees all and he knows all. Moreover, those who fight against us are only human. They don't possess the supernatural ability that God has.

My God has ordained shame for our enemies, and pleasantness for those who believe.

Daily Prayer

Most Gracious and Heavenly Father,

I love the Lord, my God, with all my heart and with all my soul and with all my strength and with all my mind, and I love my neighbor as myself. Luke 10:27 *On the glorious splendor of your majesty and on your wonderful works, I meditate.* Psalm 145:5

As the deer pants for water, so I long for you, O God. I thirst for God, the living God. Where can I find him to come and stand before him? Psalm 42: 1-2

But you, Lord, are a shield around me; you are my glory, the one who holds my head high. Psalm 3:3 *You perform great and wonderful deeds, for you alone are God. Teach me your ways, O Lord, that I may live according to your truth! Grant me purity of heart, so that I may honor you. With all my heart I will praise you. O Lord, my God. I will give Glory to your name forever!* Psalm 86:10-12

I know just what to do for God has made me see and understand. Isaiah 28:26

O give thanks to the Lord, for he is good; for his mercy endures forever. Let the redeemed of the Lord say so, whom he has redeemed from the hand of the enemy and gathered out of the lands, from the east and from the west, from the north and from the south. They wandered in the wilderness in a solitary way, they found no city to dwell in. Hungry and thirsty, their soul fainted in them. Then they cried unto the Lord in their trouble and he delivered them out of their distresses. And he led them forth by the right way, that they might go to a city of habitation. Oh that men would praise the Lord for his goodness, and his wonderful works to the children of men. Psalm 107:1-8

For yours, O Lord, is the greatness and the power and the glory and the victory and the majesty, for all that is in the heavens and in the earth is yours. Yours is the kingdom, O Lord, you are exalted as head above all. I Chronicles 29:11

In Jesus' Name, Amen

Sing to the Lord

I love you, Lord, my strength.

Psalm 18:1

The Lord, my God is awesome in power and wonderfully strong. He has looked upon my situation and carried me safely to a large place filled with his glory. My heart is filled with gratitude and his song is on my lips, for my enemies pursued me.

I CRIED UNTO GOD AND HE HEARD ME. HE RESPONDED. OH HOW MEN SHOULD PRAISE HIM, GIVE HIM GLORY BECAUSE GOD IS FAITHFUL. HE SEES AND HE KNOWS, AND THERE IS NO SECRET BEFORE HIM. THE LORD IS MY

MY GOD

STRENGTH AND MY SALVATION, MY HEART HEARS AND IT IS GLAD.

The Lord is my rock, my fortress and my deliverer; my God is my rock, in whom I take refuge, my shield and the horn of my salvation, my stronghold.

Psalm 18:2

When we consider God, we must realize that God sees all and he knows all. He has gone before us to make every crooked place straight. He knows the end from the beginning. God is not only faithful, he is well-able to fight our battles. We need only be still and honor him with our whole hearts and our beings. Anything that is not straight, God will straighten it up. Anyone who is trying to hurt us, God will course correct. The Lord is strong and mighty, mighty in battle and he is for us.

He reached down from on high and took hold of me; he drew me out of deep waters. He rescued me from my powerful enemy, from my foes, who were too strong for me. They confronted me in the day of my disaster, but the Lord was my support. He brought me out into a spacious place; he rescued me because he delighted in me. The Lord has dealt with me according to my righteousness; according to the cleanness of my hands he has rewarded me.

Psalm 18:16-20

When we come to God for help and we have been faithful, living a life he has ordained, God will bless us.

MY GOD TURNS DARKNESS INTO LIGHT, WITH HIS HELP, I CAN ADVANCE AGAINST A TROOP, WITH MY GOD I CAN SCALE A WALL. PSALM 18:29

Daily Prayer

Most Gracious and Heavenly Father,

I love the Lord, my God, with all my heart and with all my soul and with all my strength and with all my mind, and I love my neighbor as myself. *Luke 10:27* On the glorious splendor of your majesty and on your wonderful works, I meditate. *Psalm 145:5*

As the deer pants for water, so I long for you, O God. I thirst for God, the living God. Where can I find him to come and stand before him? *Psalm 42:1-2*

But you, Lord, are a shield around me; you are my glory, the one who holds my head high. *Psalm 3:3* You perform great and wonderful deeds, for you alone are God. Teach me your ways, O Lord, that I may live according to your truth! Grant me purity of heart, so that I may honor you. With all my heart I will praise you. O Lord, my God. I will give Glory to your name forever!
Psalm 86:10-12

I know just what to do for God has made me see and understand. *Isaiah 28:26*

O give thanks to the Lord, for he is good; for his mercy endures forever. Let the redeemed of the Lord say so, whom he has redeemed from the hand of the enemy and gathered out of the lands, from the east and from the west, from the north and from the south. They wandered in the wilderness in a solitary way, they found no city to dwell in. Hungry and thirsty, their soul fainted in them. Then they cried unto the Lord in their trouble and he delivered them out of their distresses. And he led them forth by the right way, that they might go to a city of habitation. Oh that men would praise the Lord for his goodness, and his wonderful works to the children of men.
Psalm 107:1-8

For yours, O Lord, is the greatness and the power and the glory and the victory and the majesty, for all that is in the heavens and in the earth is yours. Yours is the kingdom, O Lord, you are exalted as head above all.
I Chronicles 29:11

In Jesus' Name, Amen

mooretoread.com

Consider God's Promise

But Mary treasured up all these things and pondered them in her heart.

Luke 2:19

At the onset of Luke 2, Mary was nine months pregnant, unmarried, and headed to Bethlehem to register for a census with a man who loved her fiercely, but whom was not the father of her child.

For Mary, life was difficult and becoming more challenging by the minute. Yet, in the back of her mind, she remembered what the angel of God revealed to her before she became pregnant.

The angel told her,

"Don't be afraid, Mary. You have found favor with God. You will become pregnant, give birth to a son, and name him Jesus. He will be a great man and will be called the Son of the Most High. The Lord God will give him the throne of his ancestor David. Your son will be king of Jacob's people forever, and his kingdom will never end."

Mary asked the angel, "How can this be? I'm a virgin."

The angel answered her, "The Holy Spirit will come to you, and the power of the Most High will overshadow you. Therefore, the holy child developing inside you will be called the Son of God.

"Elizabeth, your relative, is six months pregnant with a son in her old age. People said she couldn't have a child. But nothing is impossible for God."

Mary answered, "I am the Lord's servant. Let everything you've said happen to me."

Then the angel left her.

Luke 1:30-38

Mary continued to consider what God promised her throughout Jesus' life. From the moment he was born, Mary pondered when the shepherds came to honor him and confessed what the angels told them. Mary pondered as she and Joseph were approached in the temple with the baby Jesus, when

Simeon, a man of God confessed that the Holy Spirit revealed to him that he would meet the Messiah, and he knew that Jesus was in deed the Son of God. Mary continued to ponder when later Jesus was found with the doctors and leaders in the temple, doing his "father's" business.

You see, God made Mary a promise, and along the path of raising Jesus, she witnessed confirmation after confirmation. She may not have had the support of others in her belief, but she nonetheless believed God. She trusted God, and rather than broadcast it, she simply pondered each revelation in her heart.

These revelations became treasures to her, precious moments that allowed her to acknowledge that her living was not in vain.

MY GOD SPEAKS AND HIS WORDS WILL NOT FAIL, AS WE BELIEVE HE WILL SEND US REVELATIONS OF TRUTH THAT WE TOO CAN PONDER IN OUR HEARTS.

Daily Prayer

Most Gracious and Heavenly Father,

I love the Lord, my God, with all my heart and with all my soul and with all my strength and with all my mind, and I love my neighbor as myself. Luke 10:27 *On the glorious splendor of your majesty and on your wonderful works, I meditate.* Psalm 145:5

As the deer pants for water, so I long for you, O God. I thirst for God, the living God. Where can I find him to come and stand before him? Psalm 42:1-2

But you, Lord, are a shield around me; you are my glory, the one who holds my head high. Psalm 3:3 *You perform great and wonderful deeds, for you alone are God. Teach me your ways, O Lord, that I may live according to your truth! Grant me purity of heart, so that I may honor you. With all my heart I will praise you. O Lord, my God. I will give Glory to your name forever!* Psalm 86:10-12

I know just what to do for God has made me see and understand. Isaiah 28:26

O give thanks to the Lord, for he is good; for his mercy endures forever. Let the redeemed of the Lord say so, whom he has redeemed from the hand of the enemy and gathered out of the lands, from the east and from the west, from the north and from the south. They wandered in the wilderness in a solitary way, they found no city to dwell in. Hungry and thirsty, their soul fainted in them. Then they cried unto the Lord in their trouble and he delivered them out of their distresses. And he led them forth by the right way, that they might go to a city of habitation. Oh that men would praise the Lord for his goodness, and his wonderful works to the children of men. Psalm 107:1-8

For yours, O Lord, is the greatness and the power and the glory and the victory and the majesty, for all that is in the heavens and in the earth is yours. Yours is the kingdom, O Lord, you are exalted as head above all. I Chronicles 29:11

In Jesus' Name, Amen

Day 12

Daybreak

And the lookout shouted, "Day after day, my lord, I stand on the watchtower; every night I stay at my post. Look, here comes a man in a chariot with a team of horses. And he gives back the answer: 'Babylon has fallen, has fallen! All the images of its gods lie shattered on the ground!'"

Isaiah 21:8-9

God is warning us to be alert, and pay attention. While our relief is en route, there is still a battle before us. God has seen the work of our enemy, heard the taunting words of those who wish to rule embattered people, and he has spoken. Help is on the way. But it is still a season off, therefore we must continue the work we have been assigned by the Holy Spirit to do. For the end of the enemy's reign is yet to come.

My GOD

God has a way of allowing us to know he sees us. He has shown us over and over again that he listens to the cries of his people. He has shown us that not only does he hear us, but that he personally will come and see what is transpiring.

When the people of Sodom and Gomorrah were sinning so much that those who lived amongst them cried out to God, God came to personally witness their oppression. When Moses led the Israelites from the slavery of the Egyptians, God went with them in a cloud by day and fire by night, he was not far off as they journeyed in the wilderness and spoke with Moses face-to-face. When Gideon and his people were taken advantage of by the Midianites, God heard their cry and allowed Gideon to rise up as a mighty man of valour. When the slave woman subjected to the rape of her master for the purpose of birthing an heir was shunned by the very woman who subjected her to such treatment, God heard her child's cry in the desert and assured her that he would be with them.

GOD KNOWS WHAT WE EXPERIENCE AND HE HEARS OUR CRIES. HE WILL NOT TURN HIS HEAD FOREVER, BUT INSTEAD IS PAYING CLOSE ATTENTION AND KNOWS THE WAY OF THE ENEMY. GOD DOES NOT SLEEP OR SLUMBER.

> This is what the Lord says to me: "Within one year, as a servant bound by contract would count it, all the splendor of Kedar will come to an end. The survivors of the archers, the warriors of Kedar, will be few." The Lord, the God of Israel, has spoken.
>
> Isaiah 21:16-17

The reign of our enemies, those who worship false gods, is in view, it is on the horizon, our God has spoken.

MY GOD IS OUR REFUGE AND STRENGTH, A VERY PRESENT HELP IN THE TIME OF TROUBLE. PSALM 46:1

Daily Prayer

Most Gracious and Heavenly Father,

I love the Lord, my God, with all my heart and with all my soul and with all my strength and with all my mind, and I love my neighbor as myself. Luke 10:27
On the glorious splendor of your majesty and on your wonderful works, I meditate. Psalm 145:5

As the deer pants for water, so I long for you, O God. I thirst for God, the living God. Where can I find him to come and stand before him? Psalm 42:1-2

But you, Lord, are a shield around me; you are my glory, the one who holds my head high. Psalm 3:3 *You perform great and wonderful deeds, for you alone are God. Teach me your ways, O Lord, that I may live according to your truth! Grant me purity of heart, so that I may honor you. With all my heart I will praise you. O Lord, my God. I will give Glory to your name forever!*
Psalm 86:10-12

I know just what to do for God has made me see and understand. Isaiah 28:26

O give thanks to the Lord, for he is good; for his mercy endures forever. Let the redeemed of the Lord say so, whom he has redeemed from the hand of the enemy and gathered out of the lands, from the east and from the west, from the north and from the south. They wandered in the wilderness in a solitary way, they found no city to dwell in. Hungry and thirsty, their soul fainted in them. Then they cried unto the Lord in their trouble and he delivered them out of their distresses. And he led them forth by the right way, that they might go to a city of habitation. Oh that men would praise the Lord for his goodness, and his wonderful works to the children of men.
Psalm 107:1-8

For yours, O Lord, is the greatness and the power and the glory and the victory and the majesty, for all that is in the heavens and in the earth is yours. Yours is the kingdom, O Lord, you are exalted as head above all.
I Chronicles 29:11

In Jesus' Name, Amen

mooretoread.com

Day 13

See and Say

The Lord said to me, "You have seen correctly, for I am watching to see that my word is fulfilled."

Jeremiah 1:13

When we receive visions or even a Word from the Lord, we are to carefully consider the message. Sometimes the message is a warning to us, other times it is a prophecy for a time to come. But we cannot receive a Word from God without being open to Him, we also will not respond appropriately if we are not careful. Even when we hear from God and are accustomed to hearing from Him, we can still miss the mark.

God calls Jeremiah to a difficult work. He is chosen to be the voice of God among a group of people who'd become hardened to God.

> Then the Lord reached out his hand and touched my mouth and said to me, "I have put my words in your mouth. See, today I appoint you over nations and kingdoms to uproot and tear down, to destroy and overthrow, to build and to plant."
>
> Jeremiah 1:9-10

Many of the Israelites had fallen into idol worship. They worshipped the work of their hands as opposed to praising and thanking God for his mercy and his grace. They refused to consider God and his will. Instead, they thought their own selves superior to the ways of God and therefore were under his judgment. It was Jeremiah's responsibility to share this message with them. But it would not be easy.

> "Get yourself ready! Stand up and say to them whatever I command you. Do not be terrified by them, or I will terrify you before them. Today I have made you a fortified city, an iron pillar and a bronze wall to stand against the whole land—against the kings of Judah, its officials, its priests and the people of

the land. They will fight against you but will not overcome you, for I am with you and will rescue you," declares the Lord.

Jeremiah 1:17-19

God has given each of us the opportunity to connect with him authentically. When we connect, God is going to share his vision, his will, and his directives. It is up to us to become not only available but willing (because God is going before us to make every crooked place straight and no matter how difficult the audience God is in control), even when he sends us to share a message that serves as conviction in the ears of the listener.

MY GOD WILL PROTECT US AS WE DO HIS WILL IN THE EARTH.

Daily Prayer

Most Gracious and Heavenly Father,

I love the Lord, my God, with all my heart and with all my soul and with all my strength and with all my mind, and I love my neighbor as myself. Luke 10:27
On the glorious splendor of your majesty and on your wonderful works, I meditate. Psalm 145:5

As the deer pants for water, so I long for you, O God. I thirst for God, the living God. Where can I find him to come and stand before him? Psalm 42:1-2

But you, Lord, are a shield around me; you are my glory, the one who holds my head high. Psalm 3:3 *You perform great and wonderful deeds, for you alone are God. Teach me your ways, O Lord, that I may live according to your truth! Grant me purity of heart, so that I may honor you. With all my heart I will praise you. O Lord, my God. I will give Glory to your name forever!*
Psalm 86:10-12

I know just what to do for God has made me see and understand. Isaiah 28:26

O give thanks to the Lord, for he is good; for his mercy endures forever. Let the redeemed of the Lord say so, whom he has redeemed from the hand of the enemy and gathered out of the lands, from the east and from the west, from the north and from the south. They wandered in the wilderness in a solitary way, they found no city to dwell in. Hungry and thirsty, their soul fainted in them. Then they cried unto the Lord in their trouble and he delivered them out of their distresses. And he led them forth by the right way, that they might go to a city of habitation. Oh that men would praise the Lord for his goodness, and his wonderful works to the children of men.
Psalm 107:1-8

For yours, O Lord, is the greatness and the power and the glory and the victory and the majesty, for all that is in the heavens and in the earth is yours. Yours is the kingdom, O Lord, you are exalted as head above all.
I Chronicles 29:11

In Jesus' Name, Amen

Perseverance is Victory

And the Lord preserved David withersoever he went.

2 Samuel 8:6b

David endured rejection and hardship before receiving his opportunity to serve as king. By experiencing arduous and tough circumstances, he developed a reliant relationship with God. He depended on God and therefore trusted him to see him through every dark moment and seemingly untenable situation. David realized that God was on his side.

In the New International Version of the Bible, this scripture reads, "And the Lord gave David victory wherever he went." 2 Samuel 8:6b

MY GOD

This is a reality we can all appreciate. Regardless of our circumstance, we can adopt and acknowledge that God is always for us. He desires that we live an abundant life, relying on him as our sole source. When we let go and let God, we can adopt the confidence of David, a mighty warrior, compassionate leader, and authentic servant of God.

In response, much like David we are to give God praise! Praise comes in many forms, but authentic worship is the most beautiful praise we can give to God. When we dedicate those things we love most to the most high, we reflect a heart that is reliant, trusting, and most importantly, in awe that leads to honor of God.

MY GOD WILL GIVE US AN UNWAVERING CONFIDENCE THAT WILL LEAD US TO VICTORY AS WE PERSEVERE EVERY CIRCUMSTANCE.

Daily Prayer

Most Gracious and Heavenly Father,

I love the Lord, my God, with all my heart and with all my soul and with all my strength and with all my mind, and I love my neighbor as myself. Luke 10:27
On the glorious splendor of your majesty and on your wonderful works, I meditate. Psalm 145:5

As the deer pants for water, so I long for you, O God. I thirst for God, the living God. Where can I find him to come and stand before him? Psalm 42:1-2

But you, Lord, are a shield around me; you are my glory, the one who holds my head high. Psalm 3:3 *You perform great and wonderful deeds, for you alone are God. Teach me your ways, O Lord, that I may live according to your truth! Grant me purity of heart, so that I may honor you. With all my heart I will praise you. O Lord, my God. I will give Glory to your name forever!*
Psalm 86:10-12

I know just what to do for God has made me see and understand. Isaiah 28:26

O give thanks to the Lord, for he is good; for his mercy endures forever. Let the redeemed of the Lord say so, whom he has redeemed from the hand of the enemy and gathered out of the lands, from the east and from the west, from the north and from the south. They wandered in the wilderness in a solitary way, they found no city to dwell in. Hungry and thirsty, their soul fainted in them. Then they cried unto the Lord in their trouble and he delivered them out of their distresses. And he led them forth by the right way, that they might go to a city of habitation. Oh that men would praise the Lord for his goodness, and his wonderful works to the children of men.
Psalm 107:1-8

For yours, O Lord, is the greatness and the power and the glory and the victory and the majesty, for all that is in the heavens and in the earth is yours. Yours is the kingdom, O Lord, you are exalted as head above all.
1 Chronicles 29:11

In Jesus' Name, Amen

Day 15

His Glory Shall Be Seen Upon Thee

Arise, shine; for thy light is come, and the glory of the Lord is risen upon thee.

Isaiah 60:1

When we accept Jesus Christ as our Lord and Savior, we accept a gift that cannot be earned. There is nothing we could ever do to deserve the non-negotiable benefits that come with being an adopted child of the Almighty Father. Yet, this is gifted to us by association and adoption into the family of Jesus Christ.

When we hear young children sing, 'This little light of

mine, I am going to let it shine...' we can recognize that we too have his glorious light shining upon us each day.

> *For, behold, the darkness shall cover the earth, and gross darkness the people: but the Lord shall arise upon thee, and his glory shall be seen upon thee. And the Gentiles shall come to thy light, and kings to the brightness of thy rising.*
>
> Isaiah 60:2-3

There is something special, unique, and necessary that only the children of God can bring to a situation. What the children of God bring is the presence of the Holy Spirit, we invite God into the conversation, allow him to breathe on it, place his fingerprints upon it, and therefore bless it.

> *The glory of Lebanon shall come unto thee, the fir tree, the pine tree, and the box together, to beautify the place of my sanctuary; and I will make the place of my feet glorious.*
>
> Isaiah 60:13

Where God is blessings flow. Abundance, peace, strength,

fortitude, joy, mercy, grace, protection, provision, and direction are non-negotiable benefits that only God can provide. People seek abundance, peace, strength, fortitude, joy, mercy, grace, protection, provision, and direction which God has given to those who share his light with others. It is the presence of God on our lives that attracts the masses and it is the gift of God, through us by the blood of Jesus Christ and the power of the Holy Spirit that we are able to share it.

Before we became conduits of God's love, mercy, grace, and message, we were in darkness, lost and misunderstood. But it is the love of God, the sacrifice of Christ, and the Holy Spirit who has made our lives whole and complete, ready to be of service to others and ready to share the love and message of God.

Whereas thou has been forsaken and hated, so that no man went through thee, I will make thee an eternal excellency, a joy of many generations.

Isaiah 60:15

MY GOD WILL SHINE HIS LIGHT UPON US THAT WE MAY BECOME LIGHT FOR OTHERS.

Daily Prayer

Most Gracious and Heavenly Father,

I love the Lord, my God, with all my heart and with all my soul and with all my strength and with all my mind, and I love my neighbor as myself. *Luke 10:27* On the glorious splendor of your majesty and on your wonderful works, I meditate. *Psalm 145:5*

As the deer pants for water, so I long for you, O God. I thirst for God, the living God. Where can I find him to come and stand before him? *Psalm 42: 1-2*

But you, Lord, are a shield around me; you are my glory, the one who holds my head high. *Psalm 3:3* You perform great and wonderful deeds, for you alone are God. Teach me your ways, O Lord, that I may live according to your truth! Grant me purity of heart, so that I may honor you. With all my heart I will praise you. O Lord, my God. I will give Glory to your name forever!
Psalm 86:10-12

I know just what to do for God has made me see and understand. *Isaiah 28:26*

O give thanks to the Lord, for he is good; for his mercy endures forever. Let the redeemed of the Lord say so, whom he has redeemed from the hand of the enemy and gathered out of the lands, from the east and from the west, from the north and from the south. They wandered in the wilderness in a solitary way, they found no city to dwell in. Hungry and thirsty, their soul fainted in them. Then they cried unto the Lord in their trouble and he delivered them out of their distresses. And he led them forth by the right way, that they might go to a city of habitation. Oh that men would praise the Lord for his goodness, and his wonderful works to the children of men.
Psalm 107:1-8

For yours, O Lord, is the greatness and the power and the glory and the victory and the majesty, for all that is in the heavens and in the earth is yours. Yours is the kingdom, O Lord, you are exalted as head above all.
I Chronicles 29:11

In Jesus' Name, Amen

Day 16

Wherever I Go

There above it stood the Lord, and he said: "I am the Lord, the God of your father Abraham and the God of Isaac. I will give you and your descendants the land on which you are lying. Your descendants will be like the dust of the earth, and you will spread out to the west and to the east, to the north and to the south. All peoples on earth will be blessed through you and your offspring. I am with you and will watch over you wherever you go, and I will bring you back to this land. I will not leave you until I have done what I have promised you."

Genesis 28:13-15

God often calls us to go where we have never been and to do what we've never done. But he will always be with us. Jacob was called to go and find a wife and as he embarked on his journey, he was met by the Lord in a dream. God made him a promise and he makes the same promise to those who commit

their lives to him, that he will always be with us.

> WHEN WE ARE CALLED TO AN ASSIGNMENT BY GOD IT IS OUR RESPONSIBILITY TO RESPOND WITH OBEDIENCE. OBEDIENCE IS EASIER WHEN WE TRUST GOD. IT IS MORE DIFFICULT WHEN WE KNOW WHO WE ARE (AT OUR BEST A FILTHY RAG) AND UNDERSTAND THAT GOD IS STILL CALLING US. WE OBEY, BUT WE DO SO WITH A CLOAK OF SHAME.

Before Jacob left on his journey, he and his mother devised a plan to steal his older brother's birthright. But even without the plan, it was a right his brother forfeit in a moment of weakness. Yet still, Jacob was in the position to be blessed beyond his ability to comprehend because of the blessing his father gave him. So as he embarked on his journey, these thoughts had to be in the back of his mind. Then as he rested during his journey, Jacob is met by God in a dream and honestly, he found it dreadful to be in such a holy place with such a muddled past.

But God was still calling him into the blessing, and the Lord even took the time to reassure him, before he arrived at his destination, that he was not only going to bless him, but also his seed that came after. So rather than run because he felt unworthy of the calling, he created a memorial altar and renamed that place to remind him and his descendants that this was a Holy Place where God had blessed him.

No matter where we are in life, or what we have done, as long as we have and continue to dedicate our lives to God, he will be with us wherever we go. It is important that we too create a memorial of sorts to remember when the Lord changed our lives in such a prominent way.

And I am convinced that nothing can ever separate us from God's love. Neither death nor life, neither angels nor demons, neither our fears for today nor our worries about tomorrow—not even the powers of hell can separate us from God's love. No power in the sky above or in the earth below—indeed, nothing in all creation will ever be able to separate us from the love of God that

 is revealed in Christ Jesus our Lord.

MY GOD WILL NEVER LET ANYTHING SEPARATE ME FROM HIM, HE LOVES THOSE WHO LOVE AND APPRECIATE HIM, NOW AND FOREVERMORE.

Daily Prayer

Most Gracious and Heavenly Father,

I love the Lord, my God, with all my heart and with all my soul and with all my strength and with all my mind, and I love my neighbor as myself. *Luke 10:27* On the glorious splendor of your majesty and on your wonderful works, I meditate. *Psalm 145:5*

As the deer pants for water, so I long for you, O God. I thirst for God, the living God. Where can I find him to come and stand before him? *Psalm 42: 1-2*

But you, Lord, are a shield around me; you are my glory, the one who holds my head high. *Psalm 3:3* You perform great and wonderful deeds, for you alone are God. Teach me your ways, O Lord, that I may live according to your truth! Grant me purity of heart, so that I may honor you. With all my heart I will praise you. O Lord, my God. I will give Glory to your name forever!
Psalm 86:10-12

I know just what to do for God has made me see and understand. *Isaiah 28:26*

O give thanks to the Lord, for he is good; for his mercy endures forever. Let the redeemed of the Lord say so, whom he has redeemed from the hand of the enemy and gathered out of the lands, from the east and from the west, from the north and from the south. They wandered in the wilderness in a solitary way, they found no city to dwell in. Hungry and thirsty, their soul fainted in them. Then they cried unto the Lord in their trouble and he delivered them out of their distresses. And he led them forth by the right way, that they might go to a city of habitation. Oh that men would praise the Lord for his goodness, and his wonderful works to the children of men.
Psalm 107:1-8

For yours, O Lord, is the greatness and the power and the glory and the victory and the majesty, for all that is in the heavens and in the earth is yours. Yours is the kingdom, O Lord, you are exalted as head above all.
1 Chronicles 29:11

In Jesus' Name, Amen

Day 17

Under His Wings

> "I have heard how you left your father and mother and your own land to live here among complete strangers. May the Lord, the God of Israel, under whose wings you have come to take refuge, reward you fully for what you have done."
>
> Ruth 2: 11b-12

When Ruth was married, she spent time learning about God under the spiritual guidance of her mother-in-law. When her father-in-law and husband passed away, only the women in the family were left. There were no children in the household and nothing to keep them in their current city. Naomi, Ruth's mother-in-law, decided she wanted to go home to her native land. Ruth, who'd grown to love Naomi, but more so, the God she served, decided she was going to follow her.

 GOD

When they arrived to Naomi's hometown, they were penniless and without a way to feed themselves. Ruth decided she would go and collect the scraps of food leftover from collected harvests in fields where she could find grace.

Ruth garnered a lot of attention, for when the owner of the field where she worked asked about her, the servants not only knew who she was, they also knew her story.

Boaz was fond of her. Not only was she a humble hard-worker, but she was also beautiful and courageous. Her courage to leave all that she knew to follow her heart for God was commendable, to humbly take care of the person that once cared for her, was also worth noting.

GOD SEES EVERYTHING WE DO. HE KNOWS HOW HARD WE WORK AND ALL THAT WE DO TO ENSURE WE ARE SERVING WITH EXCELLENCE. HE KNOWS OUR DOWNSITTING AND OUR STANDING UP, THERE IS NOTHING

THAT IS OUT OF HIS VIEW. WHEN WE FIND OURSELVES IN SITUATIONS LIKE RUTH AND NAOMI, WHERE OUR BACK IS AGAINST THE WALL AND WE ARE DOING ALL WE CAN TO MAKE IT RIGHT, WE CAN KNOW THAT GOD HAS US BENEATH THE SHELTER OF HIS WINGS. WE ARE SAFE FROM HARM, WHETHER IT SEEMS THAT WAY OR NOT.

Have mercy on me, O God, have mercy! I look to you for protection. I will hide beneath the shadow of your wings until the danger passes by.

Psalm 57:1

MY GOD IS PROTECTING ME BENEATH THE SHADOW OF HIS WINGS, THERE IS NOTHING AND NO ONE WHO IS ABLE TO PENETRATE HIS HEDGE OF PROTECTION AROUND ME.

Daily Prayer

Most Gracious and Heavenly Father,

I love the Lord, my God, with all my heart and with all my soul and with all my strength and with all my mind, and I love my neighbor as myself. Luke 10:27
On the glorious splendor of your majesty and on your wonderful works, I meditate. Psalm 145:5

As the deer pants for water, so I long for you, O God. I thirst for God, the living God. Where can I find him to come and stand before him? Psalm 42: 1-2

But you, Lord, are a shield around me; you are my glory, the one who holds my head high. Psalm 3:3 *You perform great and wonderful deeds, for you alone are God. Teach me your ways, O Lord, that I may live according to your truth! Grant me purity of heart, so that I may honor you. With all my heart I will praise you. O Lord, my God. I will give Glory to your name forever!*
Psalm 86:10-12

I know just what to do for God has made me see and understand. Isaiah 28:26

O give thanks to the Lord, for he is good; for his mercy endures forever. Let the redeemed of the Lord say so, whom he has redeemed from the hand of the enemy and gathered out of the lands, from the east and from the west, from the north and from the south. They wandered in the wilderness in a solitary way, they found no city to dwell in. Hungry and thirsty, their soul fainted in them. Then they cried unto the Lord in their trouble and he delivered them out of their distresses. And he led them forth by the right way, that they might go to a city of habitation. Oh that men would praise the Lord for his goodness, and his wonderful works to the children of men.
Psalm 107:1-8

For yours, O Lord, is the greatness and the power and the glory and the victory and the majesty, for all that is in the heavens and in the earth is yours. Yours is the kingdom, O Lord, you are exalted as head above all.
I Chronicles 29:11

In Jesus' Name, Amen

mooretoread.com

Day 18

In His Hands

Then the Lord gave me this message: "O Israel, can I not do to you as this potter has done to his clay? As the clay is in the potter's hand, so are you in my hand."

Jeremiah 18:7-8

Often times, we feel like we are in control of our lives. We choose a time to get out of bed, what we desire for breakfast, the shape of our day, and who we decide to spend time with. We choose our spouses, our educational institutions, where to buy a home and how we would like to retire.

BUT TRULY, ONLY GOD IS IN CONTROL. HE CAN SHIFT OUR LIVES IN A MOMENT. HOW WE SEE OUR WORLD CAN CHANGE DRASTICALLY WITH THE TIP OF HIS FINGER,

 # GOD

OR IN A WHISPER. BUT AT TIMES, WE FORGET THAT OUR CHOICES MATTER, OUR WORDS MATTER, OUR ACTIONS MATTER, AND WHAT WE HONOR MATTERS. GOD IS ALWAYS PAYING ATTENTION.

When we get off course, God helps us to course correct. If we are careful, paying attention to God, listening for his direction, we can get back on our feet. But if we only want to do what we desire, we can block God and refuse to hear his voice.

> "Therefore, Jeremiah, go and warn all Judah and Jerusalem. Say to them, 'This is what the Lord says: I am planning disaster for you instead of good. So turn from your evil ways, each of you, and do what is right.'"
>
> But the people replied, "Don't waste your breath. We will continue to live as we want to, stubbornly following our own evil desires."
>
> Jeremiah 18:11-12

MY GOD WILL SEND ME A WARNING WHEN I AM GOING OFF COURSE AND STEER ME IN A DIRECTION THAT IS GOOD, SAFE, AND HONORABLE—FOR MY LIFE IS IN HIS HANDS.

Daily Prayer

Most Gracious and Heavenly Father,

I love the Lord, my God, with all my heart and with all my soul and with all my strength and with all my mind, and I love my neighbor as myself. Luke 10:27 *On the glorious splendor of your majesty and on your wonderful works, I meditate.* Psalm 145:5

As the deer pants for water, so I long for you, O God. I thirst for God, the living God. Where can I find him to come and stand before him? Psalm 42:1-2

But you, Lord, are a shield around me; you are my glory, the one who holds my head high. Psalm 3:3 *You perform great and wonderful deeds, for you alone are God. Teach me your ways, O Lord, that I may live according to your truth! Grant me purity of heart, so that I may honor you. With all my heart I will praise you. O Lord, my God. I will give Glory to your name forever!*
Psalm 86:10-12

I know just what to do for God has made me see and understand. Isaiah 28:26

O give thanks to the Lord, for he is good; for his mercy endures forever. Let the redeemed of the Lord say so, whom he has redeemed from the hand of the enemy and gathered out of the lands, from the east and from the west, from the north and from the south. They wandered in the wilderness in a solitary way, they found no city to dwell in. Hungry and thirsty, their soul fainted in them. Then they cried unto the Lord in their trouble and he delivered them out of their distresses. And he led them forth by the right way, that they might go to a city of habitation. Oh that men would praise the Lord for his goodness, and his wonderful works to the children of men.
Psalm 107:1-8

For yours, O Lord, is the greatness and the power and the glory and the victory and the majesty, for all that is in the heavens and in the earth is yours. Yours is the kingdom, O Lord, you are exalted as head above all.
I Chronicles 29:11

In Jesus' Name, Amen

Day 19

Identity Crisis

"Anyone with ears to hear must listen to the Spirit and understand what he is saying to the churches."

Revelation 3:13

In the book of Revelation, chapter 3, Jesus is granting the gift of clarity via message to each of the churches in Sardis, Philadelphia, and Laodicea. His custom-tailored messages always begin with identifying who he is, as an authority, leader, Savior, and the author of our faith.

> "To the angel (divine messenger) of the church in Sardis write: These are the words of Him who has the seven Spirits of God and the seven stars:"

> Revelation 3:1a

> "And to the angel (divine messenger) of the church in Philadelphia write: These are the words of the Holy One, the True One, He who has the key [to the house] of David, He who opens and no one will [be able to] shut, and He who shuts and no one opens:

> Revelation 3:7

> "To the angel (divine messenger) of the church in Laodicea write: These are the words of the Amen, the trusted and faithful and true Witness, the Beginning and Origin of God's creation:

> Revelation 3:14

As an introduction, recognizing that we are hearing a direct word from our Lord and Savior carries a weight of distinction. Our ears perk, our attention is sharpened, and our goal is to not only hear but to obey. This is how we respond to those in authority and have the power to change our lives.

As Jesus talks to us about our behaviors (as he did with the churches) it is also very reasonable for each of us to consider the source of correction. It is not wise to ignore the authority that is set before us. It is not wise to mock or disregard their instruction.

Jesus also takes the time to carry the weight of distinction as it relates to his direct connection to God, at many times, he refers to God as "My God," indicating the personal and intimate relationship he himself has with the Father.

> *...for I have not found [any of] your deeds completed in the sight of My God...*
>
> Revelation 3:2b

> *He who overcomes [the world through believing that Jesus is the Son of God], I will make him a pillar in the temple of My God; he will most certainly never be put out of it, and I will write on him the name of My God, and the name of the city of My God, the new Jerusalem, which descends out of heaven from My God, and My [own] new name.*
>
> Revelation 3:12

THE HOLY SPIRIT GIFTED BY JESUS CHRIST CONVICTS US WHEN WE ARE ON THE WRONG PATH OR HEADED TOWARD

DANGER. IN THIS WAY, HE HELPS US TO TURN THE SHIP AND HEAD IN THE RIGHT DIRECTION. IT IS IMPORTANT TO RECOGNIZE THE AUTHORITY BY WHICH HE SPEAKS, AND THE RESTORATION OF THE RELATIONSHIP HE WISHES TO UPHOLD.

It was good for me to be afflicted so that I might learn your decrees.

Psalm 119:71

THE RELATIONSHIP THAT I HAVE WITH MY GOD IS VALUABLE AND WORTH FACING AN IDENTITY CRISIS WITH THE SERIOUSNESS IT WARRANTS.

Daily Prayer

Most Gracious and Heavenly Father,

I love the Lord, my God, with all my heart and with all my soul and with all my strength and with all my mind, and I love my neighbor as myself. ^{Luke 10:27}
On the glorious splendor of your majesty and on your wonderful works, I meditate. ^{Psalm 145:5}

As the deer pants for water, so I long for you, O God. I thirst for God, the living God. Where can I find him to come and stand before him? ^{Psalm 42:1-2}

But you, Lord, are a shield around me; you are my glory, the one who holds my head high. ^{Psalm 3:3} *You perform great and wonderful deeds, for you alone are God. Teach me your ways, O Lord, that I may live according to your truth! Grant me purity of heart, so that I may honor you. With all my heart I will praise you. O Lord, my God. I will give Glory to your name forever!*
Psalm 86:10-12

I know just what to do for God has made me see and understand. ^{Isaiah 28:26}

O give thanks to the Lord, for he is good; for his mercy endures forever. Let the redeemed of the Lord say so, whom he has redeemed from the hand of the enemy and gathered out of the lands, from the east and from the west, from the north and from the south. They wandered in the wilderness in a solitary way, they found no city to dwell in. Hungry and thirsty, their soul fainted in them. Then they cried unto the Lord in their trouble and he delivered them out of their distresses. And he led them forth by the right way, that they might go to a city of habitation. Oh that men would praise the Lord for his goodness, and his wonderful works to the children of men.
Psalm 107:1-8

For yours, O Lord, is the greatness and the power and the glory and the victory and the majesty, for all that is in the heavens and in the earth is yours. Yours is the kingdom, O Lord, you are exalted as head above all.
I Chronicles 29:11

In Jesus' Name, Amen

Day 20

For Those We Serve

Also put the Urim and the Thummim in the breastpiece, so they may be over Aaron's heart whenever he enters the presence of the Lord. Thus Aaron will always bear the means of making decisions for the Israelites over his heart before the Lord.

Exodus 28:30

The garments of the high priest were created that the high priest would be able to minister unto God. They were made by people who were wise in heart, and were created that the high priest may also receive dignity, honor, glory, and pleasant distinction.

The breastpiece was fitted with gold chains and an ephod etched with the names of the twelve children of Israel as a

memorial for God. It also bore Urim and Thummim which are believed to be diamonds encased in the ephod worn by the priest. Their purpose was a representation of "perfect light" and are often referenced when one is seeking a "rhema" word or divine guidance from God.

This perhaps, was the most important area of the high priest's garments. For it was the area by which his responsibility and accountability to God, those he served (the children of God), and himself came to bear. For when the high priest entered the Holy of Holies, as he ministered unto God, bearing upon his body a memorial of Israel, adorned with Urim and Thummim, he could inquire of the Lord with a pure heart expecting divine guidance from God. For the burden of caring justly over his people was great and it could not be done well without the guidance of the Almighty Father.

IN THE SAME WAY, AS WE ENTER OUR PRAYER CLOSET, CLOTHED WITH THE HOLY SPIRIT, GOD SEES THE BLOOD ON THE MERCY SEAT, A MEMORIAL OF JESUS CHRIST,

OUR PERFECT LIGHT, AND BLESSES US WITH DIVINE WISDOM AND GUIDANCE THAT WE MAY MAKE HOLY AND RIGHTEOUS DECISIONS CONCERNING GOD, THOSE WE SERVE, AND OURSELVES.

MY GOD WILL GRANT US ACCESS TO DIVINE WISDOM THAT ONLY HE CAN GIVE WHEN WE COMMIT TO MAKING GOOD DECISIONS FOR THOSE WE SERVE.

Daily Prayer

Most Gracious and Heavenly Father,

I love the Lord, my God, with all my heart and with all my soul and with all my strength and with all my mind, and I love my neighbor as myself. *Luke 10:27* On the glorious splendor of your majesty and on your wonderful works, I meditate. *Psalm 145:5*

As the deer pants for water, so I long for you, O God. I thirst for God, the living God. Where can I find him to come and stand before him? *Psalm 42:1-2*

But you, Lord, are a shield around me; you are my glory, the one who holds my head high. *Psalm 3:3* You perform great and wonderful deeds, for you alone are God. Teach me your ways, O Lord, that I may live according to your truth! Grant me purity of heart, so that I may honor you. With all my heart I will praise you. O Lord, my God. I will give Glory to your name forever!
Psalm 86:10-12

I know just what to do for God has made me see and understand. *Isaiah 28:26*

O give thanks to the Lord, for he is good; for his mercy endures forever. Let the redeemed of the Lord say so, whom he has redeemed from the hand of the enemy and gathered out of the lands, from the east and from the west, from the north and from the south. They wandered in the wilderness in a solitary way, they found no city to dwell in. Hungry and thirsty, their soul fainted in them. Then they cried unto the Lord in their trouble and he delivered them out of their distresses. And he led them forth by the right way, that they might go to a city of habitation. Oh that men would praise the Lord for his goodness, and his wonderful works to the children of men.
Psalm 107:1-8

For yours, O Lord, is the greatness and the power and the glory and the victory and the majesty, for all that is in the heavens and in the earth is yours. Yours is the kingdom, O Lord, you are exalted as head above all.
1 Chronicles 29:11

In Jesus' Name, Amen

Day 21

The Good Shepherd

He chose David his servant and took him from the sheep pens; from tending the sheep he brought him to be the shepherd of his people Jacob, of Israel his inheritance. And David shepherded them with integrity of heart; with skillful hands he led them.

Psalm 78:71-72

THE GOOD SHEPHERD KEEPS AN EYE ON HIS SHEEP AND GUIDES HIS FLOCK IN THE RIGHT WAY. THE GOOD SHEPHERD SACRIFICES HIMSELF FOR HIS SHEEP. THE GOOD SHEPHERD KEEPS GOD FIRST.

Psalm 78 details the displeasure and disdain God had grown to have for the Israelites. Day after day and occasion after occasion, the Israelites would fall into hardship, commit to God -

only to go back on their word.

> *Whenever God slew them, they would seek him;*
> *they eagerly turned to him again.*
>
> Psalm 78:34

The Lord knows everything about us, our standing and our sitting, he can number the hairs on our head. God knows that a hard head makes a soft behind (as my mother would say) and that sometimes a lesson learned the hard way is the best lesson of all. My God knows me, he knows what brings me joy and what makes me sad, what riles up anger, and what causes me to be filled with worry. In that knowing, he also knows what is good for me.

When I am living well, the way God intended, he chooses me to lead others. This position of leadership comes with great responsibility and mandates that I stay connected to the vine that I may hear from God in real time. God also gives us many chances to live a life that is good before him. He is a loving and merciful God.

He guided them safely, so they were unafraid; but the sea engulfed their enemies. And so he brought them to the border of his holy land, to the hill country his right hand had taken. He drove out nations before them and allotted their lands to them as an inheritance; he settled the tribes of Israel in their homes.

But they put God to the test and rebelled against the Most High; they did not keep his statutes.

Psalm 78:53-56

BUT WHEN WE SIN, INTENTIONALLY, OVER AND OVER AGAIN, REGARDLESS OF HOW MANY TIMES GOD HAS COME TO SAVE US, HE WILL ALLOW US TO REACH A PLACE OF DESPAIR.

Like their ancestors they were disloyal and faithless, as unreliable as a faulty bow. They angered him with their high places; they aroused his jealousy with their idols. When God heard them, he was furious; he rejected Israel completely.

Psalm 78:57-59

As a young man, David learned many lessons about how

to handle responsibility and the care of others. As a shepherd, he was given the authority and responsibility to keep his flocks safe. During this season, he learned to commune with God, to spend quality time with God, and he developed an ear for God. David loved God dearly and desired greatly to please him.

As the Israelites were running amuck wreaking havoc on the generations that were to follow by teaching their children the worship of idols, David was learning about God, how to be strong, courageous, gentle, and understanding. He was becoming a man after God's own heart.

> Then the Lord awoke as from sleep, as a warrior wakes from the stupor of wine.
>
> Psalm 78:65

God was done placating the Israelites and allowing his mercy to be taken for granted. He gave them over to their desires which in turn devoured what was left of their lives. After a season, God shifted and entrusted leadership of the Israelites to the tribe of Judah, which landed directly upon David. David was intelligent, honest, authentic, passionate, and chosen by God to lead his people. David was also in the lineage of Jesus Christ.

> *He built his sanctuary like the heights, like the earth that he established forever.*
>
> Psalm 78:69

Jesus Christ, our Lord and Savior is the everlasting Good Shepherd, the Prince of Peace, and our salvation.

> *"I am the good shepherd; I know my sheep and my sheep know me—just as the Father knows me and I know the Father—and I lay down my life for the sheep. I have other sheep that are not of this sheep pen. I must bring them also. They too will listen to my voice, and there shall be one flock and one shepherd. The reason my Father loves me is that I lay down my life—only to take it up again. No one takes it from me, but I lay it down of my own accord. I have authority to lay it down and authority to take it up again. This command I received from my Father."*
>
> John 10:14-18

MY GOD WILL ENTRUST US WITH LEADERSHIP WHEN WE HONOR HIM WITH OUR LIVES AND WALK WITH

INTEGRITY OF HEART, JUST AS HE HAS GIVEN US OUR GOOD SHEPHERD JESUS CHRIST, WE TOO WILL BECOME GOOD SHEPHERDS FOR THOSE WE HAVE BEEN LED TO SERVE.

Daily Prayer

Most Gracious and Heavenly Father,

I love the Lord, my God, with all my heart and with all my soul and with all my strength and with all my mind, and I love my neighbor as myself. *Luke 10:27* On the glorious splendor of your majesty and on your wonderful works, I meditate. *Psalm 145:5*

As the deer pants for water, so I long for you, O God. I thirst for God, the living God. Where can I find him to come and stand before him? *Psalm 42: 1-2*

But you, Lord, are a shield around me; you are my glory, the one who holds my head high. *Psalm 3:3* You perform great and wonderful deeds, for you alone are God. Teach me your ways, O Lord, that I may live according to your truth! Grant me purity of heart, so that I may honor you. With all my heart I will praise you. O Lord, my God. I will give Glory to your name forever!
Psalm 86:10-12

I know just what to do for God has made me see and understand. *Isaiah 28:26*

O give thanks to the Lord, for he is good; for his mercy endures forever. Let the redeemed of the Lord say so, whom he has redeemed from the hand of the enemy and gathered out of the lands, from the east and from the west, from the north and from the south. They wandered in the wilderness in a solitary way, they found no city to dwell in. Hungry and thirsty, their soul fainted in them. Then they cried unto the Lord in their trouble and he delivered them out of their distresses. And he led them forth by the right way, that they might go to a city of habitation. Oh that men would praise the Lord for his goodness, and his wonderful works to the children of men.
Psalm 107:1-8

For yours, O Lord, is the greatness and the power and the glory and the victory and the majesty, for all that is in the heavens and in the earth is yours. Yours is the kingdom, O Lord, you are exalted as head above all.
I Chronicles 29:11

In Jesus' Name, Amen

Day 22

The Lord Will Answer

Then you will call, and the Lord will answer; you will cry for help, and he will say: Here am I. If you do away with the yoke of oppression, with the pointing finger and malicious talk, and if you spend yourselves in behalf of the hungry and satisfy the needs of the oppressed, then your light will rise in the darkness, and your night will become like the noonday.

Isaiah 58:9-10

THERE IS A SPECIFIC POSTURE THAT IS REQUIRED TO HEAR FROM GOD. WE CANNOT PRETEND WITH GOD. HE SEES RIGHT THROUGH US.

For the word of God is quick, and powerful, and sharper than any twoedged sword, piercing even to the dividing

asunder of soul and spirit, and of the joints and marrow, and is a discerner of the thoughts and intents of the heart.

Hebrews 4:12 - 13

We cannot come before God expecting him to act when we have not completely surrendered to his will. He desires a sincere, authentic, and repentant heart. He desires to spend intimate time with us. He expects us to honor his will before our own.

If we are careful to obey God and commit to his way of life, not only will he hear us when we call, he will answer us. This means we honor the Sabbath and keep it holy, that our fasts lead to spiritual awakening rather than public acknowledgement, and that our hearts are open and generous to those with the greatest need among us. Then when we call on God, he will answer us.

"If you keep your feet from breaking the Sabbath and from doing as you please on my holy day, if you call the Sabbath a delight and the Lord's holy day honorable, and if you honor it by not going your own way and not doing as you please or speaking idle words, then you will find your joy in the Lord, and I will cause you to ride in triumph on the heights of the land and to feast on the inheritance of your father Jacob." The mouth of the Lord has spoken.

Isaiah 58:13-14

MY GOD WILL HEAR AND BLESS THOSE WHO HONOR HIM IN SPIRIT AND TRUTH.

Daily Prayer

Most Gracious and Heavenly Father,

I love the Lord, my God, with all my heart and with all my soul and with all my strength and with all my mind, and I love my neighbor as myself. *Luke 10:27* On the glorious splendor of your majesty and on your wonderful works, I meditate. *Psalm 145:5*

As the deer pants for water, so I long for you, O God. I thirst for God, the living God. Where can I find him to come and stand before him? *Psalm 42:1-2*

But you, Lord, are a shield around me; you are my glory, the one who holds my head high. *Psalm 3:3* You perform great and wonderful deeds, for you alone are God. Teach me your ways, O Lord, that I may live according to your truth! Grant me purity of heart, so that I may honor you. With all my heart I will praise you. O Lord, my God. I will give Glory to your name forever!
Psalm 86:10-12

I know just what to do for God has made me see and understand. *Isaiah 28:26*

O give thanks to the Lord, for he is good; for his mercy endures forever. Let the redeemed of the Lord say so, whom he has redeemed from the hand of the enemy and gathered out of the lands, from the east and from the west, from the north and from the south. They wandered in the wilderness in a solitary way, they found no city to dwell in. Hungry and thirsty, their soul fainted in them. Then they cried unto the Lord in their trouble and he delivered them out of their distresses. And he led them forth by the right way, that they might go to a city of habitation. Oh that men would praise the Lord for his goodness, and his wonderful works to the children of men.
Psalm 107:1-8

For yours, O Lord, is the greatness and the power and the glory and the victory and the majesty, for all that is in the heavens and in the earth is yours. Yours is the kingdom, O Lord, you are exalted as head above all.
I Chronicles 29:11

In Jesus' Name, Amen

Day 23

Separate & Protected

> 'Then Haman said to King Xerxes, "There is a certain people dispersed among the peoples in all the provinces of your kingdom who keep themselves separate. Their customs are different from those of all other people, and they do not obey the king's laws; it is not in the king's best interest to tolerate them.'
>
> Esther 3:8

When you make God your head, the enemy will whisper in secret places about you. It is not that you are wrong, evil, or have ill-intentions, but it is the fact that you are standing in the most honorable position our enemy used to have, you are giving God praise! Your lifestyle reflects a sincere praise unto God, your worship reflects a heart that is bowed before him, and your choices reflect that you honor God above all others.

My GOD

Thou hast been in Eden the garden of God; every precious stone was thy covering: the sardius, topaz, and the diamond, the beryl, the onyx, and the jasper, the sapphire, the emerald, and the carbuncle, and gold; the workmanship of thy taborets and of thy pipes was prepared in thee in the day that thou wast created. Thou art the anointed cherub that covereth, and I have set thee so; thou wast upon the holy mountain of God; thou hast walked up and down in the midst of the stones of fire. Thou wast perfect in thy ways from the day that thou wast created, till iniquity was found in thee.

Ezekiel 28:13 - 15

Before Satan was cast down, he was the most adorned angel and had one of the most amazing jobs any of us could ask for, he was in charge of praise to God. Therefore God made him beautiful and equipped him for the work that was set before him. But Satan wanted to receive praise. He didn't want to be a pipeline by which praise flowed to God, he desired to be the recipient. Unfortunately, he did not realize he was not equipped nor did he understand the responsibility of what he desired. He was cast down and we can imagine that the rejection of God is a far worse position than being the pipeline of his praise.

> SATAN SET HIMSELF AS AN ENEMY TO ANYONE WHO HONORED GOD. IN FACT, HE MADE IT HIS TOP PRIORITY TO REMIND GOD THAT THOSE WHOM GOD LOVED WERE SINNERS.

> *And I heard a loud voice in heaven, saying, "Now the salvation and the power and the kingdom of our God and the authority of his Christ have come, for the accuser of our brothers has been thrown down, who accuses them day and night before our God.*
>
> *Revelation 12:10*

In the book of Esther, when Mordecai saved the king's life from those who plotted against him, the enemy of God plotted to kill not only Mordecai but every person of Jewish heritage who worshipped God. This was done so that evil was repaid for good.

> *Day after day they spoke to him but he refused to comply. Therefore they told Haman about it to see whether Mordecai's behavior would be tolerated, for he had told them he was a Jew.*
>
> *Esther 3:4*

MY GOD

We cannot be confused when we find ourselves in circumstances or situations we did not cause, nor can we lose our confidence in God. When Haman was told that Mordecai refused to comply, he convinced the king that it was in his best interest to get rid of every Jew. When the Jews heard the news, they were afraid and perplexed. But the king and Haman sat down to drink and be merry as if there were reason to celebrate.

> And the letters were sent by posts into all the king's provinces, to destroy, to kill, and to cause to perish all Jews, both young and old, little children and women in one day, even upon the thirteenth day of the twelfth month, which is the month of Adar, and to take the spoil of them for plunder. The copy of the writing, to be given for a commandment in every province, was published unto all people, that they should be ready against that day. The posts went out, being hastened by the king's commandment, and the decree was given in the palace of Shushan. And the king and Haman sat down to drink, but the city of Shushan was perplexed.
>
> Esther 3:13-15

Without the betrayal there can be no victory. When the enemy thinks that they have outwitted you, or destroyed you because you refuse to bow down to their authority (over the authority of God) or succumb to their will God will raise up a standard. The Lord will protect us.

> *Finally, be strong in the Lord and in the strength of his might. Put on the whole armor of God, that you may be able to stand against the schemes of the devil. For we do not wrestle against flesh and blood, but against the rulers, against the authorities, against the cosmic powers over this present darkness, against the spiritual forces of evil in the heavenly places.*
>
> *Ephesians 6:10-12*

MY GOD WILL KEEP US SEPARATE AND PROTECTED FROM THE SECRET PLOTS OF THE ENEMY, THEREFORE WE MUST KEEP OUR CONFIDENCE AND HOPE IN THE LORD.

Daily Prayer

Most Gracious and Heavenly Father,

I love the Lord, my God, with all my heart and with all my soul and with all my strength and with all my mind, and I love my neighbor as myself. Luke 10:27
On the glorious splendor of your majesty and on your wonderful works, I meditate. Psalm 145:5

As the deer pants for water, so I long for you, O God. I thirst for God, the living God. Where can I find him to come and stand before him? Psalm 42:1-2

But you, Lord, are a shield around me; you are my glory, the one who holds my head high. Psalm 3:3 *You perform great and wonderful deeds, for you alone are God. Teach me your ways, O Lord, that I may live according to your truth! Grant me purity of heart, so that I may honor you. With all my heart I will praise you. O Lord, my God. I will give Glory to your name forever!*
Psalm 86:10-12

I know just what to do for God has made me see and understand. Isaiah 28:26

O give thanks to the Lord, for he is good; for his mercy endures forever. Let the redeemed of the Lord say so, whom he has redeemed from the hand of the enemy and gathered out of the lands, from the east and from the west, from the north and from the south. They wandered in the wilderness in a solitary way, they found no city to dwell in. Hungry and thirsty, their soul fainted in them. Then they cried unto the Lord in their trouble and he delivered them out of their distresses. And he led them forth by the right way, that they might go to a city of habitation. Oh that men would praise the Lord for his goodness, and his wonderful works to the children of men.
Psalm 107:1-8

For yours, O Lord, is the greatness and the power and the glory and the victory and the majesty, for all that is in the heavens and in the earth is yours. Yours is the kingdom, O Lord, you are exalted as head above all.
I Chronicles 29:11

In Jesus' Name, Amen

mooretoread.com

Day 24

Run

Beware of dogs, beware of evil workers, beware of the Concision.

Philippians 3:2

Most of us work tirelessly our entire lives to bless our families, be successful, and to leave a legacy of truth and wisdom for those who may follow us. But all of these things are nothing if Christ is not at the center, and while we may feel or even seem to others as intelligent, we are mindless and unable to truly comprehend life's meaning if we lean only on what we can glean from our own minds.

WE HAVE BEEN CREATED IN THE LIKENESS OF GOD AND THEREFORE ARE SMART, INTELLIGENT, LOVING,

AND THOUGHTFUL. BUT IT WAS JESUS ALONE, WHO SACRIFICED HIS LIFE THAT WE MAY GAIN ETERNAL LIFE.

So we must know without a shadow of a doubt that God is, God will, and God does. It is our belief in the Great I Am that allows us to be successful, to live a life that is able to bless others, to achieve our hopes and dreams while doing the very will of God in the process.

The dogs of this world are those who bark without bite, inciting riots without participating in them. The evil workers are those who do their best to convince us that God is not real and that Jesus did not die for us. Concision is the practice of removing history to encourage tomorrows culture, rather than acknowledging that history will repeat itself, so it is best to be reminded of it.

I want to know Christ—yes, to know the power of his resurrection and participation in his sufferings, becoming like him in his death, and so, somehow, attaining to the resurrection from the dead. Not that I have already obtained all this, or have already arrived at my goal, but I press on to take hold of that for which Christ Jesus took hold of me.

Philippians 3:10-12

Regardless of how good, intelligent, spiritually astute or disciplined we are, we are only what we are and where we are because God allowed it. It is not because we live perfect, neat, and responsible lives, but because Jesus Christ, the Son of God, the Living Word, has sacrificed his life that we may live in peace, receiving mercy and grace in our time of need, guided by the Holy Spirit. Let us run, run the race that God designed, and to do it with excellence as Jesus has taught us by the power of the Holy Spirit.

Finally, my brethren, rejoice in the Lord.

Philippians 3:1a

BY FAITH, MY GOD, THE LORD, JESUS CHRIST, HAS SACRIFICED ALL THAT I MAY LIVE, THEREFORE, BY FAITH I TOO WILL SACRIFICE ALL THAT I MAY LIVE AS HE DID, DESIRING ONLY TO DO HIS WILL.

Daily Prayer

Most Gracious and Heavenly Father,

I love the Lord, my God, with all my heart and with all my soul and with all my strength and with all my mind, and I love my neighbor as myself. Luke 10:27 *On the glorious splendor of your majesty and on your wonderful works, I meditate.* Psalm 145:5

As the deer pants for water, so I long for you, O God. I thirst for God, the living God. Where can I find him to come and stand before him? Psalm 42:1-2

But you, Lord, are a shield around me; you are my glory, the one who holds my head high. Psalm 3:3 *You perform great and wonderful deeds, for you alone are God. Teach me your ways, O Lord, that I may live according to your truth! Grant me purity of heart, so that I may honor you. With all my heart I will praise you. O Lord, my God. I will give Glory to your name forever!*
Psalm 86:10-12

I know just what to do for God has made me see and understand. Isaiah 28:26

O give thanks to the Lord, for he is good; for his mercy endures forever. Let the redeemed of the Lord say so, whom he has redeemed from the hand of the enemy and gathered out of the lands, from the east and from the west, from the north and from the south. They wandered in the wilderness in a solitary way, they found no city to dwell in. Hungry and thirsty, their soul fainted in them. Then they cried unto the Lord in their trouble and he delivered them out of their distresses. And he led them forth by the right way, that they might go to a city of habitation. Oh that men would praise the Lord for his goodness, and his wonderful works to the children of men.
Psalm 107:1-8

For yours, O Lord, is the greatness and the power and the glory and the victory and the majesty, for all that is in the heavens and in the earth is yours. Yours is the kingdom, O Lord, you are exalted as head above all.
I Chronicles 29:11

In Jesus' Name, Amen

mooretoread.com

Consider, ASK, and Be Wise

Therefore, whoever heareth these sayings of mine, and doeth them I will liken him unto a wise man, which built his house upon a rock.

Matthew 7:24

It is very easy to judge our neighbor and their response to a situation when we have not had the burden of walking in their shoes. It is much harder to judge ourselves, especially when we have four more fingers pointing back at us. But we must consider our thoughts, our words, and our actions because while private amongst others they are visible before God and he is measuring the intentions of the heart.

MY GOD

We must also be careful not to give the most beautiful parts of ourselves to those who will not appreciate them. Sometimes, what we give is devalued by the receiver and stomped on as if it were worthless. This is not a healthy outcome for either party but is especially hurtful to the giver and destroys trust among friends.

As my mother used to say, "A closed mouth will not get fed." We must learn to ask God for what we need, and when we pray, we must believe that we have received it. For our God stands ready to answer our prayers, especially when we seek him with our whole heart and knock at his door. However, what we ask for, we must also be willing to give and God loves a cheerful giver, so it is best not to give if you do not desire to do so. But we must remember, with the same measure we give, it will be given to us, pressed down and shaken together, running over it will come back to us.

As we consider our lives, it is very important that we keep

God first because it is not easy to go into the narrow gate of heaven. The narrow gate of heaven requires that we live a life that God ordains as it reflects our true merit of faith in Him. If we are living the life we designed and hope that God will bless it, we are attempting to enter heaven through the wide gate. It is our obedience to his will by having enough faith to trust his plan that allows us to enter the narrow gate, it is not hoping that God will confine to our will.

How do we know if we are walking in the will of God? Simply put, by our fruit. Are we producing what God has assigned us to produce? Or are we doing what makes us happy and brings us joy? A wise man will please God and then even his enemies will be at peace with him.

Finally, a wise man hears God and obeys, while a foolish man will allow the word of God to enter one ear and flow from the other without considering what God desires of their lives. The wise man has God as his rock, a solid foundation that will never fail, while the foolish man rests on his personal ability to solve his

issue, but will only find it is sinking sand.

> MY GOD TEACHES US TO BE CONSIDERATE, RESOURCEFUL, AND WISE THAT WE MAY LIVE THE LIFE THAT HE DESIGNED.

Daily Prayer

Most Gracious and Heavenly Father,

I love the Lord, my God, with all my heart and with all my soul and with all my strength and with all my mind, and I love my neighbor as myself. Luke 10:27
On the glorious splendor of your majesty and on your wonderful works, I meditate. Psalm 145:5

As the deer pants for water, so I long for you, O God. I thirst for God, the living God. Where can I find him to come and stand before him? Psalm 42:1-2

But you, Lord, are a shield around me; you are my glory, the one who holds my head high. Psalm 3:3 *You perform great and wonderful deeds, for you alone are God. Teach me your ways, O Lord, that I may live according to your truth! Grant me purity of heart, so that I may honor you. With all my heart I will praise you. O Lord, my God. I will give Glory to your name forever!*
Psalm 86:10-12

I know just what to do for God has made me see and understand. Isaiah 28:26

O give thanks to the Lord, for he is good; for his mercy endures forever. Let the redeemed of the Lord say so, whom he has redeemed from the hand of the enemy and gathered out of the lands, from the east and from the west, from the north and from the south. They wandered in the wilderness in a solitary way, they found no city to dwell in. Hungry and thirsty, their soul fainted in them. Then they cried unto the Lord in their trouble and he delivered them out of their distresses. And he led them forth by the right way, that they might go to a city of habitation. Oh that men would praise the Lord for his goodness, and his wonderful works to the children of men.
Psalm 107:1-8

For yours, O Lord, is the greatness and the power and the glory and the victory and the majesty, for all that is in the heavens and in the earth is yours. Yours is the kingdom, O Lord, you are exalted as head above all.
I Chronicles 29:11

In Jesus' Name, Amen

As God Commands

Noah did everything just as God commanded him.

Genesis 6:22

Have you ever bought furniture online and had to put it together at home? I have learned that if you do not follow the explicit instructions the end result will not be as you imagined it should.

Much like furniture, skipping steps when God instructs us means that we are going to miss something important, even critical and it could adversely impact what God intended. As you know, those 'little' missed steps can result in doors not closing

properly, drawers not shutting, and perhaps even worse. How much more are we impacted when we do not follow God's explcit command.

Well, Noah was a man that found favor with God because he was paying attention to God. Many on the Earth were chasing after their own heart's desires without listening to God. Their lack of attention caused them to miss the important notification that God was about to end the world! Only Noah was paying attention to God, he had his eyes affixed, his ears open, and his heart in a posture conducive to trust and have faith.

WE ONLY TRUST GOD WHEN WE KNOW HIM OR KNOW ENOUGH ABOUT HIM TO COMMIT IN OUR HEARTS, "WHATEVER YOU SAY GOD, I WILL DO."

God gave Noah detailed instructions and the bible says that Noah followed every command.

MY GOD WILL REVEAL SECRETS, SIGNS, AND WONDERS TO THOSE WHO ARE PAYING ATTENTION, WITH OPEN EARS AND HEARTS READY TO TRUST AND SERVE.

Daily Prayer

Most Gracious and Heavenly Father,

I love the Lord, my God, with all my heart and with all my soul and with all my strength and with all my mind, and I love my neighbor as myself. Luke 10:27 *On the glorious splendor of your majesty and on your wonderful works, I meditate.* Psalm 145:5

As the deer pants for water, so I long for you, O God. I thirst for God, the living God. Where can I find him to come and stand before him? Psalm 42:1-2

But you, Lord, are a shield around me; you are my glory, the one who holds my head high. Psalm 3:3 *You perform great and wonderful deeds, for you alone are God. Teach me your ways, O Lord, that I may live according to your truth! Grant me purity of heart, so that I may honor you. With all my heart I will praise you. O Lord, my God. I will give Glory to your name forever!* Psalm 86:10-12

I know just what to do for God has made me see and understand. Isaiah 28:26

O give thanks to the Lord, for he is good; for his mercy endures forever. Let the redeemed of the Lord say so, whom he has redeemed from the hand of the enemy and gathered out of the lands, from the east and from the west, from the north and from the south. They wandered in the wilderness in a solitary way, they found no city to dwell in. Hungry and thirsty, their soul fainted in them. Then they cried unto the Lord in their trouble and he delivered them out of their distresses. And he led them forth by the right way, that they might go to a city of habitation. Oh that men would praise the Lord for his goodness, and his wonderful works to the children of men. Psalm 107:1-8

For yours, O Lord, is the greatness and the power and the glory and the victory and the majesty, for all that is in the heavens and in the earth is yours. Yours is the kingdom, O Lord, you are exalted as head above all. 1 Chronicles 29:11

In Jesus' Name, Amen

Day 27

The Cause was of God

So the king did not listen to the people, for this turn of events was from God, to fulfill the word the Lord had spoken to Jeroboam son of Nebat through Ahijah the Shilonite.

2 Chronicles 10:15

GOD IS IN CONTROL.

HE PAYS ATTENTION TO EVERY DETAIL.

God visited King Solomon twice in his lifetime, God loved Solomon and blessed him immensely. Solomon was one of the offspring of King David, a man after God's own heart. David walked with God faithfully all of his days. But Solomon was not the same as his father. Solomon had seven hundred wives and often found himself worshipping their gods. This angered God

who had been so generous and kind to Solomon. But because God made David a promise, and assured David that there would always be a son of his bloodline to rule in Jerusalem, God honored his word.

Solomon passed away and his son Rehoboam became king. But God remembered the acts of Solomon and had already ordained another to rule ten of the twelve kingdoms once ruled by Solomon. God raised up enemies against his son and those enemies did as God had ordained. They pressed Rehoboam and caused hardship for his kingdom, but one in particular, Jeroboam led many in Jerusalem to revolt against Rehoboam.

This was the plan of God. It was ordained and as it should be. For Solomon led his sons to believe that their rulership was the crown of their glory, when in reality, it was their commitment and honor of God which provided favor, success, discernment, and wisdom.

When we honor God, as a young King Solomon set out to

do, God will open doors for us. But when we believe it is because of who we are, what we do, and how we serve that doors are opened, we fail, falter, and fall. King Rehoboam considered himself worthy of honor, but God did not agree. The Lord did as he planned and ripped the kingdoms from his hand.

God is our Heavenly Father, he does not only father one, he fathers us all. So if the choices of one cause hardship to many, especially one who is in leadership of many, God has to shift the light that many can be blessed with his presence, his gifts, his love, and his appreciation.

MY GOD WILL CAUSE A SHIFT IN LEADERSHIP, WHEN LEADERS FAIL THE MANY.

Daily Prayer

Most Gracious and Heavenly Father,

I love the Lord, my God, with all my heart and with all my soul and with all my strength and with all my mind, and I love my neighbor as myself. Luke 10:27
On the glorious splendor of your majesty and on your wonderful works, I meditate. Psalm 145:5

As the deer pants for water, so I long for you, O God. I thirst for God, the living God. Where can I find him to come and stand before him? Psalm 42:1-2

But you, Lord, are a shield around me; you are my glory, the one who holds my head high. Psalm 3:3 *You perform great and wonderful deeds, for you alone are God. Teach me your ways, O Lord, that I may live according to your truth! Grant me purity of heart, so that I may honor you. With all my heart I will praise you. O Lord, my God. I will give Glory to your name forever!*
Psalm 86:10-12

I know just what to do for God has made me see and understand. Isaiah 28:26

O give thanks to the Lord, for he is good; for his mercy endures forever. Let the redeemed of the Lord say so, whom he has redeemed from the hand of the enemy and gathered out of the lands, from the east and from the west, from the north and from the south. They wandered in the wilderness in a solitary way, they found no city to dwell in. Hungry and thirsty, their soul fainted in them. Then they cried unto the Lord in their trouble and he delivered them out of their distresses. And he led them forth by the right way, that they might go to a city of habitation. Oh that men would praise the Lord for his goodness, and his wonderful works to the children of men.
Psalm 107:1-8

For yours, O Lord, is the greatness and the power and the glory and the victory and the majesty, for all that is in the heavens and in the earth is yours. Yours is the kingdom, O Lord, you are exalted as head above all.
I Chronicles 29:11

In Jesus' Name, Amen

Day 28

Day and Night

Keep this Book of the Law always on your lips; meditate on it day and night, so that you may be careful to do everything written in it. Then you will be prosperous and successful.

Joshua 1:8

Joshua steadfastly studied Moses. When Moses met with God in the tent of meeting, Joshua was there. When Moses received the Ten Commandments, Joshua was there. We don't hear from Joshua in those moments, but we get glimpses of his presence in the text, therefore we know Joshua was an astute apprentice.

When it was time for him to become a leader, he was ready. He'd done the work, studied the process, developed his own

relationship with God and was found prepared to manage the next leg in the journey, entrance into the Promised Land.

But before Joshua could address the people, God encouraged him.

> "Moses my servant is dead. Now then, you and all these people, get ready to cross the Jordan River into the land I am about to give to them—to the Israelites. I will give you every place where you set your foot, as I promised Moses. Your territory will extend from the desert to Lebanon, and from the great river, the Euphrates—all the Hittite country—to the Mediterranean Sea in the west. No one will be able to stand against you all the days of your life. As I was with Moses, so I will be with you; I will never leave you nor forsake you. Be strong and courageous, because you will lead these people to inherit the land I swore to their ancestors to give them."
>
> Joshua 1: 2-6

WHEN WE ARE READY TO GO TO THE NEXT LEVEL, THERE ISN'T ANYTHING OR ANYONE THAT CAN STAND IN THE WAY. PROMOTION COMES FROM GOD. BUT THE WAY TO SUCCESS IS NOT PAVED EASILY AND IT REQUIRES DISCIPLINE. IT REQUIRES THE DISCIPLINE TO SEEK THE LIVING GOD DAY AND NIGHT, AT ALL TIMES, NO MATTER

WHERE WE ARE OR WHAT WE PLAN TO DO.

> "Be strong and very courageous. Be careful to obey all the law my servant Moses gave you; do not turn from it to the right or to the left, that you may be successful wherever you go. Keep this Book of the Law always on your lips; meditate on it day and night, so that you may be careful to do everything written in it. Then you will be prosperous and successful. Have I not commanded you? Be strong and courageous. Do not be afraid; do not be discouraged, for the Lord your God will be with you wherever you go."
>
> Joshua 1: 7-9

Just as God prepared Joshua for what was next, he is also preparing us. We must sit at his feet day and night, soaking in his presence, seeking his direction, and studying his Word.

THERE IS AN HONOR WE BESTOW UPON GOD WHEN WE SEEK HIS FACE DAY AND NIGHT, AND WHEN WE HAVE PROVEN OURSELVES SINCERE, WE SEE HIS HAND FILLED WITH SUCCESS AND PROSPERITY.

Daily Prayer

Most Gracious and Heavenly Father,

I love the Lord, my God, with all my heart and with all my soul and with all my strength and with all my mind, and I love my neighbor as myself. Luke 10:27
On the glorious splendor of your majesty and on your wonderful works, I meditate. Psalm 145:5

As the deer pants for water, so I long for you, O God. I thirst for God, the living God. Where can I find him to come and stand before him? Psalm 42: 1-2

But you, Lord, are a shield around me; you are my glory, the one who holds my head high. Psalm 3:3 *You perform great and wonderful deeds, for you alone are God. Teach me your ways, O Lord, that I may live according to your truth! Grant me purity of heart, so that I may honor you. With all my heart I will praise you. O Lord, my God. I will give Glory to your name forever!*
Psalm 86:10-12

I know just what to do for God has made me see and understand. Isaiah 28:26

O give thanks to the Lord, for he is good; for his mercy endures forever. Let the redeemed of the Lord say so, whom he has redeemed from the hand of the enemy and gathered out of the lands, from the east and from the west, from the north and from the south. They wandered in the wilderness in a solitary way, they found no city to dwell in. Hungry and thirsty, their soul fainted in them. Then they cried unto the Lord in their trouble and he delivered them out of their distresses. And he led them forth by the right way, that they might go to a city of habitation. Oh that men would praise the Lord for his goodness, and his wonderful works to the children of men.
Psalm 107:1-8

For yours, O Lord, is the greatness and the power and the glory and the victory and the majesty, for all that is in the heavens and in the earth is yours. Yours is the kingdom, O Lord, you are exalted as head above all.
1 Chronicles 29:11

In Jesus' Name, Amen

Where is Your God?

My tears have been my food day and night, while people say to me all day long, "Where is your God?"

Psalm 42:3

There are times when everyone around you will look at you as though you don't belong in elite spaces. Yet, there you sit, welcomed by the host, just as they were. Some may feel more entitled, postured, or tenured and feel as though they have the right to judge, question, or doubt who you are.

Regardless of their opinion, the question seems to linger. Where is your God?

What they know is that you worship the King of Kings and Lord of Lords. They know you honor God with your life - but look at you. And in those moments, if you stand in the same position and try to see yourself from their vantage point, you may too begin to question, where is my God?

> I say to God my Rock, "Why have you forgotten me? Why must I go about mourning, oppressed by the enemy?" My bones suffer mortal agony as my foes taunt me, saying to me all day long, "Where is your God?"
>
> Psalm 42:9-10

But we must not allow the opinion of others to dictate or negate the power that lies within us by the power of the Holy Spirit through Christ. No we must not stand in agreement with those who question our validity to be in the room.

INSTEAD WE MUST FIND OUR IDENTITY IN CHRIST, THE KING OF KINGS AND THE LORD OF LORDS. IT IS FAR BETTER TO ALIGN OURSELVES WITH THE WILL OF THE ONE, TRUE, AND LIVING GOD THAN TO GAIN THE

FRUITLESS ATTRIBUTES OF WHAT THE WORLD DESIRES.

Why, my soul, are you downcast? Why so disturbed within me? Put your hope in God, for I will yet praise him, my Savior and my God.

Psalm 42:11

MY GOD WILL SHINE HIS LIGHT UPON ME IN THE DARKNESS AND I WILL SING HIS PRAISE FOR HE IS MY GOD.

Daily Prayer

Most Gracious and Heavenly Father,

I love the Lord, my God, with all my heart and with all my soul and with all my strength and with all my mind, and I love my neighbor as myself. Luke 10:27
On the glorious splendor of your majesty and on your wonderful works, I meditate. Psalm 145:5

As the deer pants for water, so I long for you, O God. I thirst for God, the living God. Where can I find him to come and stand before him? Psalm 42:1-2

But you, Lord, are a shield around me; you are my glory, the one who holds my head high. Psalm 3:3 *You perform great and wonderful deeds, for you alone are God. Teach me your ways, O Lord, that I may live according to your truth! Grant me purity of heart, so that I may honor you. With all my heart I will praise you. O Lord, my God. I will give Glory to your name forever!* Psalm 86:10-12

I know just what to do for God has made me see and understand. Isaiah 28:26

O give thanks to the Lord, for he is good; for his mercy endures forever. Let the redeemed of the Lord say so, whom he has redeemed from the hand of the enemy and gathered out of the lands, from the east and from the west, from the north and from the south. They wandered in the wilderness in a solitary way, they found no city to dwell in. Hungry and thirsty, their soul fainted in them. Then they cried unto the Lord in their trouble and he delivered them out of their distresses. And he led them forth by the right way, that they might go to a city of habitation. Oh that men would praise the Lord for his goodness, and his wonderful works to the children of men. Psalm 107:1-8

For yours, O Lord, is the greatness and the power and the glory and the victory and the majesty, for all that is in the heavens and in the earth is yours. Yours is the kingdom, O Lord, you are exalted as head above all. I Chronicles 29:11

In Jesus' Name, Amen

Day 30

It's Easier to Start a War than End One

Now Ben-Hadad the king of Syria gathered all his forces together; thirty-two kings were with him, with horses and chariots. And he went up and besieged Samaria, and made war against it.

I Kings 20:1

The enemy likes to pick on those who are weak. The enemy makes the mistake in believing that those who appear to be weak are simply meat for the fodder.

Then the messengers came back and said, "Thus speaks Ben-Hadad, saying, 'Indeed I have sent to you, saying, "You shall deliver to me your silver and your gold, your wives and your children"; but I will send my servants to you tomorrow about this time, and they shall search your

house and the houses of your servants. And it shall be, that whatever is pleasant in your eyes, they will put it in their hands and take it.'"

I Kings 20:5-6

But God.

GOD IS ACUTELY AWARE OF EVERY STRATEGY THE ENEMY EMPLOYS. GOD KNOWS THE END FROM THE BEGINNING. GOD KNOWS THE THAT THE ENEMY UNDERESTIMATES ALL THAT YOU ARE AND ALL THAT YOU ARE CAPABLE OF DOING. IN FACT, THE ENEMY BELIEVES THAT HE CAN PLUNDER WHATEVER VALUE YOU HAVE AND TAKE IT FOR HIMSELF.

So he said, "If they have come out for peace, take them alive; and if they have come out for war, take them alive."

I Kings 20:18

But God.

You see it is easier to start a war than end one - because God has the final say. It doesn't matter if the enemy has more power, resources, acumen, or strength - God has the final say!

> **BUT WE MUST SEEK GOD AND HIS GUIDANCE IN REAL-TIME. WE MUST TREAT OUR ENEMY AS THE ARE—OUR TRUE ENEMY!**

Suddenly a prophet approached Ahab king of Israel, saying, "Thus says the Lord: 'Have you seen all this great multitude? Behold, I will deliver it into your hand today, and you shall know that I am the Lord.'

So Ahab said, "By whom?"

And he said, "Thus says the Lord: 'By the young leaders of the provinces.'"

Then he said, "Who will set the battle in order?"

And he answered, "You."

I Kings 20:13-14

Our enemy underestimates us and allows his eyes to see what his head and heart cannot. By following what they see on the surface they are destroyed by what we represent in reality.

And the children of Israel were mustered and given provisions, and they went against them. Now the children of Israel encamped

before them like two little flocks of goats, while the Syrians filled the countryside. Then a man of God came and spoke to the king of Israel, and said, "Thus says the Lord: 'Because the Syrians have said, "The Lord is God of the hills, but He is not God of the valleys," therefore I will deliver all this great multitude into your hand, and you shall know that I am the Lord.'"

I Kings 20:27-28

MY GOD IS THE ENEMY OF MY ENEMY!

Daily Prayer

Most Gracious and Heavenly Father,

I love the Lord, my God, with all my heart and with all my soul and with all my strength and with all my mind, and I love my neighbor as myself. Luke 10:27 *On the glorious splendor of your majesty and on your wonderful works, I meditate.* Psalm 145:5

As the deer pants for water, so I long for you, O God. I thirst for God, the living God. Where can I find him to come and stand before him? Psalm 42:1-2

But you, Lord, are a shield around me; you are my glory, the one who holds my head high. Psalm 3:3 *You perform great and wonderful deeds, for you alone are God. Teach me your ways, O Lord, that I may live according to your truth! Grant me purity of heart, so that I may honor you. With all my heart I will praise you. O Lord, my God. I will give Glory to your name forever!*
Psalm 86:10-12

I know just what to do for God has made me see and understand. Isaiah 28:26

O give thanks to the Lord, for he is good; for his mercy endures forever. Let the redeemed of the Lord say so, whom he has redeemed from the hand of the enemy and gathered out of the lands, from the east and from the west, from the north and from the south. They wandered in the wilderness in a solitary way, they found no city to dwell in. Hungry and thirsty, their soul fainted in them. Then they cried unto the Lord in their trouble and he delivered them out of their distresses. And he led them forth by the right way, that they might go to a city of habitation. Oh that men would praise the Lord for his goodness, and his wonderful works to the children of men.
Psalm 107:1-8

For yours, O Lord, is the greatness and the power and the glory and the victory and the majesty, for all that is in the heavens and in the earth is yours. Yours is the kingdom, O Lord, you are exalted as head above all.
I Chronicles 29:11

In Jesus' Name, Amen

Make His Praise Glorious!

Oh, bless our God, you peoples! And make the voice of His praise to be heard, Who keeps our soul among the living, And does not allow our feet to be moved.

Psalm 66:8-9

To be loved by God is akin to the love of no other. For God in his infinite wisdom, abundant love, unyielding mercy, and powerful hand holds us tightly and claims us as his own.

Therefore from the abundance of our heart, we speak! We give God an amazing praise because he is - wonderful!

My God

God never ceases to amaze me. He has given me life and life more abundantly.

His love endures forever. If we honor him with our lives and do not hold sin in our heart, he will hear us when we pray and he will answer our prayer.

Blessed be God, who has not turned away my prayer, nor His mercy from me!

Psalm 66:20

My God is my God. He is my everything! Whether I sit in mire clay, or cascade a mountain top, wade in shallow waters, or venture to the deep, my God is with me wherever I go and I am blessed.

He deserves all the praise!

Daily Prayer

Most Gracious and Heavenly Father,

I love the Lord, my God, with all my heart and with all my soul and with all my strength and with all my mind, and I love my neighbor as myself. Luke 10:27 *On the glorious splendor of your majesty and on your wonderful works, I meditate.* Psalm 145:5

As the deer pants for water, so I long for you, O God. I thirst for God, the living God. Where can I find him to come and stand before him? Psalm 42:1-2

But you, Lord, are a shield around me; you are my glory, the one who holds my head high. Psalm 3:3 *You perform great and wonderful deeds, for you alone are God. Teach me your ways, O Lord, that I may live according to your truth! Grant me purity of heart, so that I may honor you. With all my heart I will praise you. O Lord, my God. I will give Glory to your name forever!*
Psalm 86:10-12

I know just what to do for God has made me see and understand. Isaiah 28:26

O give thanks to the Lord, for he is good; for his mercy endures forever. Let the redeemed of the Lord say so, whom he has redeemed from the hand of the enemy and gathered out of the lands, from the east and from the west, from the north and from the south. They wandered in the wilderness in a solitary way, they found no city to dwell in. Hungry and thirsty, their soul fainted in them. Then they cried unto the Lord in their trouble and he delivered them out of their distresses. And he led them forth by the right way, that they might go to a city of habitation. Oh that men would praise the Lord for his goodness, and his wonderful works to the children of men.
Psalm 107:1-8

For yours, O Lord, is the greatness and the power and the glory and the victory and the majesty, for all that is in the heavens and in the earth is yours. Yours is the kingdom, O Lord, you are exalted as head above all.
1 Chronicles 29:11

In Jesus' Name, Amen

About the Author

At the age of 9, Stephanie was molested by a friend of my family. In high school, she held the hand of a friend as he died from a fatal gun shot wound… As an adult, she was the victim of a violent acquaintance rape. Subsequently, she struggled with personal demons. But when she sought the Lord and his Word, her life was forever changed.

Give God ALL the Glory!

He is and will always be the head of my life. He is my joy, my strength, my everything.
My constant prayer is to be a perfect conduit of his message and love.

Stephanie was born in Muskogee, Oklahoma. She graduated from Putnam City North High School in 1994. She was married for 16 years. She is the mother of 3 beautiful daughters, and has a grandson named Levi. She graduated with her Associates in Technology, a Bachelor of Arts in Communications, and a Master of Arts in Communication with an emphasis in Political Communication.

She holds several design and technology certifications and has won numerous awards in that area. Stephanie has worked in television, print and web media for more than 16 years.

She is the owner of Moore Marketing and Communications. Her company offers strategic marketing and communication plans, media purchases, public relations, writing services, print services, graphic design and web design. Stephanie has also served as a poltical consultant for Governor, Lt. Governor, State Representative, Mayoral and City Council candidates.

Stephanie has created and sponsored teen etiquette and leadership programs for young ladies and young men. The program for young ladies is called, She's a BOSSE (A Beautiful Oasis of Success, Style and Elegance) and the young man's program is called Grindaholix: Young Men on the Rise.

To date, Stephanie has authored 37 books, 26 of which are daily devotionals.
To learn more, visit mooretoread.com.